GEOLOGY OF THE EASTERN COAST

INVESTIGATE HOW THE EARTH WAS FORMED

with **15** PROJECTS

CYNTHIA LIGHT BROWN & KATHLEEN BROWN

Illustrated by Eric Baker

~ Titles in the *Build It Yourself* Series ~

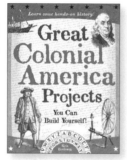

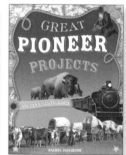

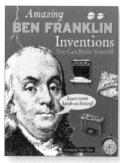

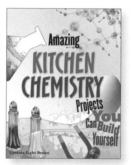

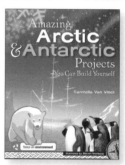

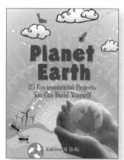

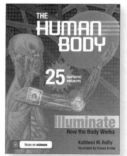

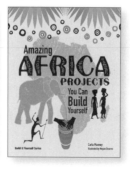

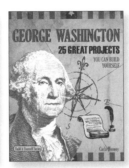

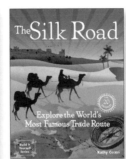

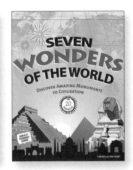

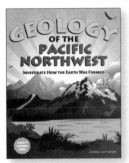

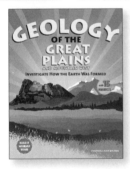

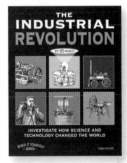

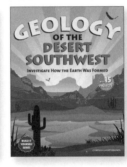

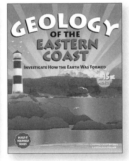

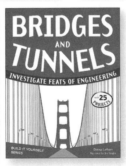

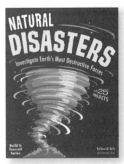

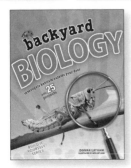

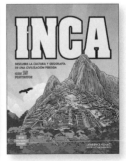

green press

INITIATIVE

Nomad Press is committed to preserving ancient forests and natural resources. We elected to print *Geology of the Eastern Coast: Investigate How the Earth Was Formed* on 4,507 lbs. of Williamsburg Recycled 30 percent offset.

Nomad Press made this paper choice because our printer, Sheridan Books, is a member of Green Press Initiative, a nonprofit program dedicated to supporting authors, publishers, and suppliers in their efforts to reduce their use of fiber obtained from endangered forests. For more information, visit **www.greenpressinitiative.org**

Nomad Press
A division of Nomad Communications
10 9 8 7 6 5 4 3 2 1

This book was manufactured by Sheridan Books,
Ann Arbor, MI USA.
March 2012, Job # 334797
ISBN: 978-1-936313-87-7

Illustrations by Eric Baker
Educational Consultant Marla Conn

Questions regarding the ordering of this book should be addressed to
Independent Publishers Group
814 N. Franklin St.
Chicago, IL 60610
www.ipgbook.com

Nomad Press
2456 Christian St.
White River Junction, VT 05001
www.nomadpress.net

~CONTENTS~

Mississippi River

Appalachian Trail

Chesapeake Bay

GEOLOGY & GEOGRAPHY

The Eastern Coast is more than just the land by the ocean. The region has sweeping, majestic forests. Groundhogs live there, and snapping alligators fill the swamps in the south. And you might know about the fierce, destructive hurricanes.

But did you know the Eastern Coast also has amazing natural wonders? Have you heard of Mount Washington in New Hampshire or Chesapeake Bay in Maryland? Maybe you've visited the lower Mississippi River Delta, or the Florida Everglades. The Eastern Coast is linked from its coastline along the Atlantic Ocean to the inland Appalachian Mountain chain running from Maine to Alabama.

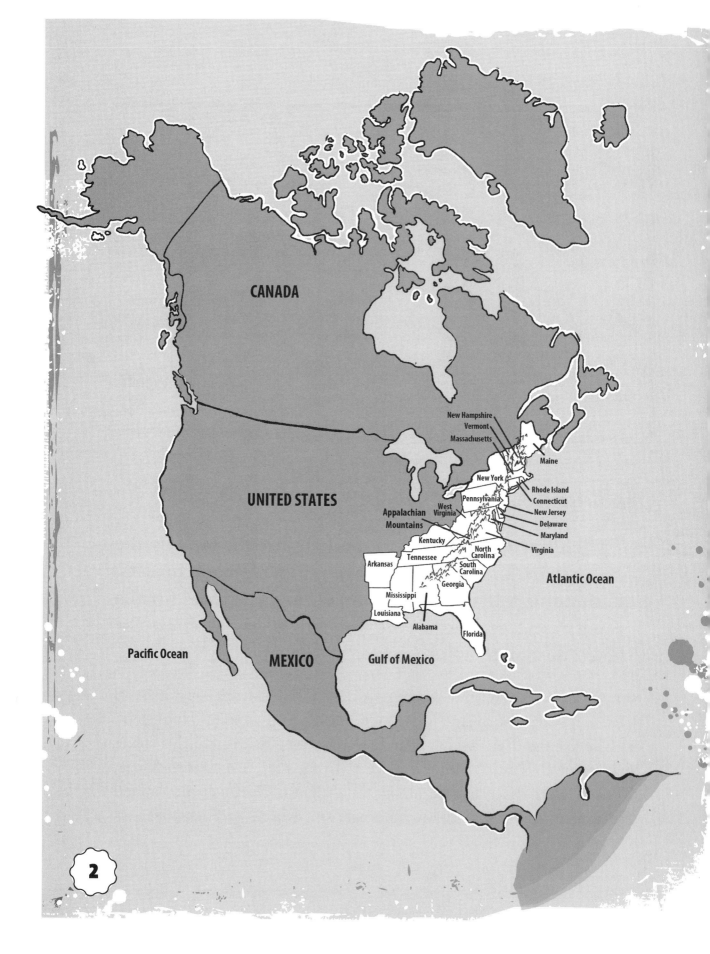

CANADA

UNITED STATES

MEXICO

Pacific Ocean

Gulf of Mexico

Atlantic Ocean

New Hampshire
Vermont
Massachusetts
Maine
New York
Rhode Island
Pennsylvania
Connecticut
New Jersey
Appalachian
Mountains
West
Virginia
Delaware
Maryland
Kentucky
Virginia
North
Carolina
Tennessee
Arkansas
South
Carolina
Georgia
Mississippi
Louisiana
Alabama
Florida

The region is a mature landscape, which means it's had a very long time to develop. Even with its old mountains and rivers, though, it's still changing all the time.

In this book, you'll learn about the **geology** and physical **geography** of the Eastern Region along the coast of the Atlantic Ocean and part of the Gulf of Mexico. You'll read about the forces that have shaped the region's mountains, plains, rivers, weather, and **ecosystems**. And you'll discover a lot of interesting facts about the area.

WORDS TO KNOW

geology: the scientific study of the history and physical nature of the earth.

geography: the study of the earth and its features, especially the shape of the land, and the effect of human activity on the earth.

ecosystem: a community of plants and animals living in the same area and relying on each other to survive.

endangered: a kind of plant or animal that is at risk of disappearing entirely.

Did you know that alligators were once **endangered**, but now number in the hundreds of thousands? Or that the Great Smoky Mountains have fireflies that flash in unison? As you read through this book, you'll get to try out experiments and projects. They will help you understand new concepts, like how rocks get folded in mountains, or how waterfalls can "move" up a river.

GEOLOGY: MORE THAN JUST ROCKS

Most people think of geology as the study of rocks. It certainly includes that, but it's much more. When you look at a rock, you can describe its color and shape. But what is even more interesting is how that rock formed and how it got to its present location. That involves seeing the big picture—the picture of the whole earth.

Geology is the scientific study of the history and physical nature of the earth. It explains how the color and shape of a rock gives clues to the history of that rock.

WORDS TO KNOW

crust: the thick, outer layer of the earth.

atmosphere: the air surrounding the earth.

hydrosphere: the earth's water, including oceans, rivers, lakes, glaciers, and water vapor in the air.

climate: the average weather of an area over a long period of time.

Geology involves the huge movements of the earth's **crust**. It also involves the systems of the **atmosphere** and **hydrosphere**, because air and water affect the breakdown and formation of rocks. And the geology of the Eastern Coast is part of the geologic story of our nation and the earth.

GEOGRAPHY: MORE THAN JUST STATES AND CAPITALS

Just as geology is about more than just rocks, geography is about more than just states and their capitals. These are important, but geography tells a bigger story. There are two parts to geography. Physical geography includes mountains, rivers, **climate**, and the shape of the land. Cultural geography is how people interact with the land. An example of cultural geography would be how trying to prevent floods can change the shape of a river. Cultural geography includes things like population, agriculture, and recreation.

This book covers the states of Arkansas, Louisiana, Mississippi, Alabama, Tennessee, Georgia, Kentucky, Florida, South Carolina, North Carolina, Virginia, West Virginia, Maryland, Pennsylvania, Delaware, New Jersey, New York, Connecticut, Rhode Island, Massachusetts, Vermont, New Hampshire, and Maine.

Come sail on the Chesapeake Bay, hike the Appalachian Trail from Maine to Georgia, and ride a raft down the Mississippi River. This beautiful land is ready and waiting to be explored—by you!

CHAPTER 1

PLATE TECTONICS
SHAPE OUR LAND AND SEA

The Atlantic and Gulf coasts gently slope down to the ocean. Farther inland, a group of mountain ranges called the Appalachian Mountains rise, almost following the line of the coast. How did these areas form and why do they look so different?

To understand the driving force behind the formation of the different landscapes in the Eastern Coast, you first need to understand **plate tectonics**.

WORDS TO KNOW

volcano: a vent in the earth's surface through which magma, ash, and gases erupt.

earthquake: a sudden movement in the outer layer of the earth. It releases stress built up from the motion of the earth's plates.

erosion: the wearing away and carrying off of materials on the earth's surface.

brittle: describes a solid that breaks when put under pressure. A blade of grass will bend, but a dry twig is brittle and will break.

mantle: the middle layer of the earth. The upper mantle, together with the crust, forms the lithosphere.

dense: tightly packed.

lithosphere: the rigid outer layer of the earth that includes the crust and the upper mantle.

Plate tectonics is the theory that the outer layer of the earth is made up of interconnected plates that move around. Together with the heat from the sun, the powerful forces inside the earth shape every landscape and ecosystem on the surface of the earth. **Volcanoes,** mountains, valleys, plains, **earthquakes**, and **erosion** all happen when and where they do because of the movement of the earth's plates. To understand plate tectonics, first let's look inside the earth.

A PEEK INSIDE

The earth may look solid and motionless, but much of it is liquid. It consists of three layers.

The crust is the thin, outer layer of the earth. This is the layer that we walk on. It's solid but **brittle**, which means that it breaks when under pressure.

The **mantle** is the layer below the crust. It is hotter and **denser** here because the temperature and pressure inside the earth increase the deeper you go. The upper mantle is brittle and solid. Together, the crust and the upper mantle form the **lithosphere**, or the hard outer layer of the earth.

The lithosphere is broken into plates. Below the plates is a layer called the **asthenosphere**. It is partially **molten** and can flow slowly without breaking—a bit like Silly Putty. The **core** is the center of the earth. It is extremely dense and made up of iron and nickel. There's an inner core, which is solid because the pressure is so great, and an outer core, which is liquid.

The core is almost as hot as the sun—about 9,000 degrees Fahrenheit (5,000 degrees Celsius)!

Did You Know?

You might have heard of the earth's plates being sections of the earth's crust. That's partly correct. The **tectonic** plates are made of the crust and the upper mantle, which together are called the lithosphere. But most people just call it the crust because it's easier to remember.

WORDS TO KNOW

asthenosphere: the semi-molten middle layer of the earth that includes the lower mantle. Much of the asthenosphere flows slowly, like Silly Putty.

molten: melted by heat to form a liquid.

core: the center of the earth, composed of the metals iron and nickel. The core has a solid inner core and a liquid outer core.

tectonic: relating to the forces that produce movement and changes in the earth's crust.

oceanic: in or from the ocean.

continental: relating to the earth's large land masses.

PLATES: THE EARTH'S PUZZLE

The hard outer layer of the earth, or lithosphere, is broken up into about 12 large sections, called tectonic plates. There are also several smaller plates. The plates fit together like a jigsaw puzzle. Most of the plates are part **oceanic** and part **continental**. For example, the North American Plate includes nearly all of North America and the western half of the Atlantic Ocean.

WORDS TO KNOW

magma: partially melted rock below the surface of the earth.

current: a constantly moving mass of liquid.

divergent boundary: where two plates are moving in opposite directions, sometimes called a rift zone. New crust forms at rift zones from the magma pushing through the crust.

rifting: when the lithosphere splits apart.

The plates are in constant slow motion!

That's because the layer just under the plates—the asthenosphere—is very hot. The heat causes the molten rocks there, called **magma**, to move around in huge rotating **currents** called convection cells. These convection cells move the plates above, which are floating like rafts on the hot goo below. The plates also help themselves move along. The older part of a plate is colder and denser. When it sinks into the mantle, it pulls the rest of the plate with it and keeps the cycle going. Plates move somewhere between 1 to 6 inches each year (2 to 15 centimeters).

ON THE EDGE

Volcanoes and earthquakes don't just happen anywhere. They're arranged in patterns. For example, there are lots of active volcanoes around the rim of the Pacific Ocean, but there are no volcanoes in Arkansas. That's because most of the action happens where one plate meets another. This is called a plate boundary. There are three different kinds of plate boundaries.

Divergent Plate Boundaries are where two plates move apart from each other. They do this because the magma beneath is pushing upward. This causes **rifting**. The hot goo pushes out and solidifies to form new rocks. Nearly all of the earth's new crust forms at divergent boundaries. An example of a divergent boundary can be found on the eastern boundary of the North American Plate, in the middle of the Atlantic Ocean.

The North American continent and the western half of the floor of the Atlantic Ocean are all part of one tectonic plate. That plate is growing, because new crust is forming at the Mid-Atlantic Ridge.

The ocean floor is spreading as lava bubbles up from below and cools to form new crust.

Convergent Plate Boundaries are where two plates collide. What happens depends on whether the plates are oceanic or continental. When an oceanic plate collides with a continental plate, volcanoes form. Because the oceanic plate is denser and thinner than the continental plate, it slides underneath the continental plate. This is called **subduction**.

As the subducted oceanic plate sinks lower, its weight pulls the rest of the plate along as well. The sinking plate encounters a lot of heat and pressure. This causes the plate to release hot gas and steam, which rises and melts the rock above. The melted rock, the magma, also rises to the surface, creating volcanoes. The Rocky Mountains in the west formed when oceanic crust subducted beneath the North American Plate and caused the crust to buckle.

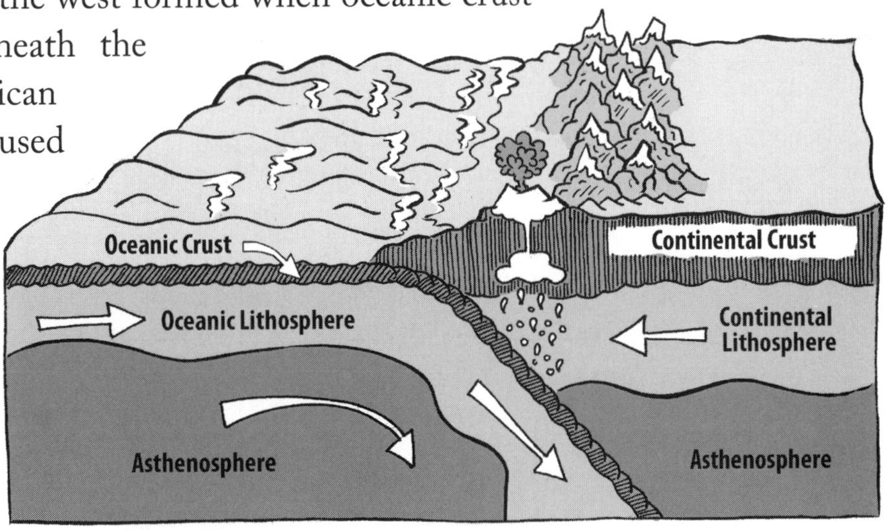

Oceanic Crust

Continental Crust

Oceanic Lithosphere

Continental Lithosphere

Asthenosphere

Asthenosphere

Oceanic-Continental Convergance

If a continental plate collides with another continental plate, they both buckle upwards, forming mountains. That's what is happening right now where the Indian Plate and the Eurasian Plate are colliding. The result is the Himalaya Mountains, which include the tallest mountain in the world, Mt. Everest.

There aren't any convergent boundaries within the Eastern Coast region, but sometimes there can be movement along old **faults**. This movement happens in an area called the New Madrid Seismic Zone, along the western edge of Tennessee and Kentucky.

Transform Plate Boundaries are where two plates grind against each other as they move side by side in opposite directions. As the plates move past each other they sometimes suddenly slip. This creates a big lurch, or earthquake. There's an old transform plate boundary that runs from New York to Alabama. This fault is buried, though, and is not nearly as active or as powerful as the more famous San Andreas Fault in California.

Hotspots are other areas of strong geologic activity, but they aren't on the edge of tectonic plates. These are volcanic regions that usually occur in the middle of a plate. They exist because extremely hot magma, probably from deep in the mantle, makes its way to the surface. There is a hotspot beneath Yellowstone National Park, where Wyoming, Idaho, and Montana meet.

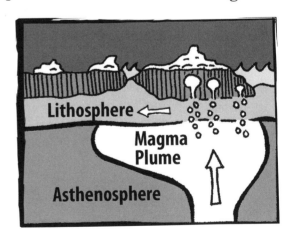

Lithosphere

Magma Plume

Asthenosphere

GIANT CONVEYOR BELT

The movement of the plates acts a bit like a giant, wide conveyor belt. This conveyor belt is like a flat escalator, used to move people or things across a long space. At divergent boundaries, magma pushes through, cools, and forms new crust.

The lithosphere is like a rigid board, though, and as two plates move apart, the other end of each plate collides with another lithosphere. At the collision point, one plate is subducted, or pushed under, and melts. So lithosphere is created on one end, and destroyed on another. Just like conveyor belts, or the stairs on an escalator, lithosphere appears on one end and disappears on the other end.

TECTONIC HISTORY OF THE EASTERN COAST

The Eastern Coast has had a varied tectonic history. Most places in the region have experienced different things happening at different times. For example, at one time, an area might have been an ocean basin receiving **sediments**. Much later, the same area might have been pushed up into mountains. The rocks often record this history, but it can be hard to sort out what happened when.

WORDS TO KNOW

sediment: loose rock particles such as sand and clay.

geologist: a scientist who studies the earth and its movements.

And sometimes, rocks have been completely removed due to erosion or subduction.

As you might guess, the farther back in time you go, the harder it is to tell what happened. Nevertheless, **geologists** have pieced together a rough picture of the tectonic past.

Did You Know?

The oldest rocks in the United States are found in northern Minnesota and northern Michigan. They are between 3.5 and 3.7 billion years old. The oldest rocks on Earth are in northern Canada, and are over 4 billion years old.

Over 2½ billion years ago, small bits of continental and oceanic crust collided and stuck together over time. This process formed the central part of North America, called the craton. In the Eastern Coast region, you can see a very small section of the ancient craton exposed in the Adirondack Mountains in northern New York State. In the rest of the region, other rocks have covered the ancient rocks.

A billion years ago, all the continents were assembled into a single continent surrounded by one giant ocean.

As North America collided with another continent along its eastern edge to form this supercontinent, called Rodinia, towering mountains were pushed up. Many of the rocks at the core of the Appalachians Mountains were formed during this time. Later, erosion removed layers of rocks in the mountains over many millions of years. Only the "roots" of the ancient mountains remained and the land was a flat rolling plain.

About 750 million years ago, Rodinia thinned and pulled apart—a bit like taffy. Volcanoes erupted and a deep basin formed along what was then the eastern edge of the continent. This is now western Virginia, North Carolina, South Carolina, eastern Tennessee, and northern Georgia.

Sediments

Water filled the basin, bringing along with it clay, silt, sand, and gravel. As the basin sank over millions of years, it left behind thick layers of sediments. These sediment layers can be seen now in the Great Smoky Mountains.

Later, inland seas flooded to the west and deposited sand, mud, and seashells. These formed a thin covering of **sedimentary rocks** over the older rocks throughout the central part of North America.

Layers of Sedimentary Rock

The process of continents colliding together and pushing the land up into mountains is called an orogeny. Around the time plants first began to appear on Earth, North America and Africa had started to come together to form a new supercontinent called Pangaea. This happened over a long period of about 250 million years, called the Appalachian Orogeny.

WORDS TO KNOW

sedimentary rock: rock formed from the compression of sediments, the remains of plants and animals, or from the evaporation of seawater.

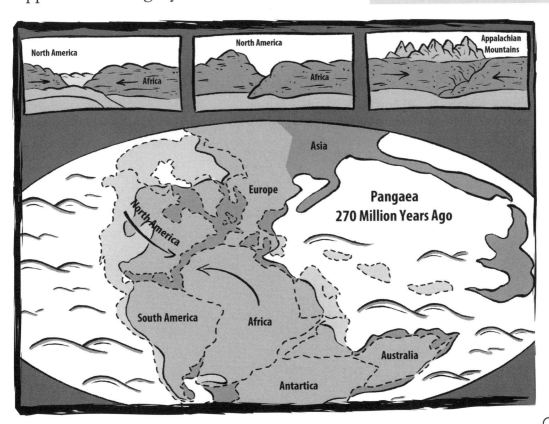

During the Appalachian Orogeny, huge blocks of continental crust piled up on top of each other. The Appalachian Mountains were pushed up as the rocks folded and faulted. As rocks were buried in the big pile-up, some changed into new **metamorphic rocks**, and others were buried deep enough that they melted. The molten rocks erupted to form volcanoes or cooled underground to form granite.

WORDS TO KNOW

metamorphic rock: rock that has been transformed by heat or pressure or both into new rock, while staying solid.

coastal plain: a flat area that is bound by the sea on one side and an area of higher elevation on the other side.

continental shelf: the border of a continent that slopes gradually under water.

glacier: a huge mass of ice and snow.

Many of those rocks are now exposed because the rock above has eroded, such as Blowing Rock in northern North Carolina and Red Top Mountain in northern Georgia.

Beginning about 240 million years ago when dinosaurs were starting to roam the land, Pangaea began rifting apart. This rifting opened up the Atlantic Ocean off the east coast of North America. Since then, the Appalachians have been eroding, with the sediments forming the **coastal plains** and the **continental shelf** all along the Atlantic and Gulf Coasts.

During the last 2 million years, **glaciers** expanded south during colder periods and shaped the northern part of the region. These glaciers covered most of New England and parts of Pennsylvania, New York, and New Jersey. Later, when Earth's climate warmed, many lakes and rivers were left as the glaciers melted.

Did You Know?

When the Appalachian Mountains were formed long ago they were probably as high as the Himalayas are today! Since then, wind, water, and ice have eroded them.

WHAT'S HAPPENING NOW?

The tectonic activity in the Eastern Coast region has been relatively quiet for a long time. You won't find active volcanoes here, and even the ancient mountains have been eroded to lower **elevations**. We are also in a warmer period in Earth's history, and glaciers have retreated north, leaving bodies of water behind. Going from east to west, this is what you'll find in the Eastern Region.

WORDS TO KNOW

elevation: height above sea level.

A Widening Atlantic Ocean: There is a divergent plate boundary near the center of the Atlantic Ocean, running from north to south. Magma is pushing up through openings to form new crust. It means that the Atlantic Ocean is actually getting wider every day. The oceanic crust to the west of this spreading center is connected to the continental crust of North America to form the North American Plate.

COLUMBUS SAILED ALMOST ALL OF THE OCEAN BLUE!

Columbus sailed the ocean blue in 1492, but he had it easy. The Atlantic Ocean is spreading apart at about ½ to 1 inch per year (up to 2½ centimeters), so there is about 33 feet in the middle of the Atlantic Ocean (10 meters) that Columbus never traveled over!

15

Coastal Plain: The entire coast along the Atlantic Ocean and the Gulf of Mexico is a stable tectonic area. Here, the oceanic crust and the continental crust are not subducting—they are slowly, but quietly, moving west together. This is called a passive continental margin. The area is low-lying and receives sediments flowing from the Appalachian Mountains. The sedimentary rocks here are very young.

Appalachian Mountains: These mountains form the backbone of the eastern United States, extending from New England to Alabama. They include the following areas, from east to west:

• Piedmont, which has rolling hills and gentle slopes stretching from New Jersey to central Alabama.

• Blue Ridge, which has the highest mountains in the East and includes the Blue Ridge Mountains, the Great Smoky Mountains, and Shenandoah National Park.

• Valley and Ridge, which is a series of long, even ridges, with long, continuous valleys in between that look almost like stripes of corduroy meeting in a V shape.

Interior Plateau: The **plateaus** just to the west of the Appalachian Mountains include the Allegheny Plateau and the Cumberland Plateau. These plateaus have been eroded in places with steep slopes.

PLATE TECTONICS: THE ORIGINAL RECYCLER

The earth has been recycling materials for over 4 billion years! Every rock you see has come from another kind of rock. And every rock you see will eventually become another one. All this recycling is because of the movement of the plates pushing everything around. To understand this recycling, first you have to know a bit about types of rocks.

There are three main types of rocks: igneous, sedimentary, and metamorphic.

Igneous Rocks have formed from the cooling of molten rock. As you go deeper beneath the surface of the earth, it becomes hotter. At around 25 miles beneath the surface (40 kilometers), it's hot enough to melt rocks. When that molten rock, called magma, comes to the surface, it cools into igneous rocks.

Sedimentary Rocks form when small particles of rock, called **sediments**, are pressed tightly together into rock. Sediments come from other rocks being eroded, or broken into smaller pieces by wind, water, ice, and gravity. Sedimentary rocks can also form from the remains of plants or animals being pressed together. When seawater evaporates, the minerals and salts in the water stay behind and can form into rock.

Metamorphic Rocks form when heat or pressure changes rocks into new rocks. Pressure, like temperature, increases as you go farther beneath the surface of the earth. If rocks are pushed under the surface, but not far enough to melt, they can be changed into new rocks without first melting.

Igneous rocks can be eroded into sediments, which then form sedimentary rocks. Those sedimentary rocks can then be buried and heated and squeezed to form metamorphic rocks. Metamorphic rocks can be pushed down into the mantle and melted, to later form igneous rocks. Or it could happen in reverse, because any type of rock can form from any type of rock.

MAKE YOUR OWN
PILLOW BASALTS

During the formation of Rodinia over a billion years ago, volcanoes erupted. When lava flowed on the ocean floor, it formed rocks called pillow basalts. You can find pillow basalts from this time at Stark's Knob in eastern New York.

CAUTION: This project involves using the oven, so get an adult to help. It's best to make these cookies on a cool, dry day. The meringue doesn't dry properly on hot, humid days.

1 Preheat the oven to 350 degrees Fahrenheit and put the oven rack in the center position (180 degrees Celsius). Line a cookie sheet with wax paper.

2 Hold an egg lightly with one hand. With the other hand, crack the eggshell firmly with the table knife.

3 Pull the eggshell apart without letting the yolk fall into the bowl. Separate the egg white by pouring the yolk back and forth between the eggshell halves, letting the egg white fall into one of the small bowls. Be careful that the yolk doesn't break.

4 When all of the white is in the bowl, put the yolk into the other small bowl to use for another cooking project, or throw it away. Pour the egg white into the large bowl. Repeat this process for the rest of the eggs so if you break a yolk on one egg, you won't ruin the whole batch.

5 Add the cream of tartar to the egg whites. Beat the mixture on high until the egg whites get foamy and form soft peaks that gently fall over when you remove the beaters.

6 Gradually add the sugar and vanilla, and add 2 or 3 drops of food coloring. Keep beating until the mixture is shiny, smooth, and stands up in a peak about 2 inches high (5 centimeters). With a spoon, gently fold in the chips.

SUPPLIES

- oven
- cookie sheet
- wax paper or parchment paper
- 3 large eggs at room temperature
- table knife
- 2 small bowls
- large metal or glass bowl
- ½ teaspoon cream of tartar
- electric mixer
- ⅔ cup fine granulated sugar (134 grams)
- ½ teaspoon vanilla
- green food coloring
- 1 cup mini chocolate or white chocolate chips (182 grams)

7 Drop teaspoon-sized blobs of the meringue onto the wax paper on the cookie sheet and place in the oven. Immediately turn off the oven and leave the cookie sheet in the oven for at least 2 hours. The meringues should look dry and stiff.

8 Clean up carefully! You don't get to lick the bowl in this recipe because raw eggs can make you sick. For the same reason, make sure you use paper towels to wipe up any spilled egg, then throw them in the trash.

What's Happening?

Pillow basalts form where cracks in the earth's crust have opened in the ocean floor and lava comes out into the water. The cold ocean water quickly cools the lava into a pillow shape. Pillow basalt is often green because of a reaction between the lava and the mineral-rich seawater. Sometimes basalt has gas bubbles and these bubbles later fill with minerals, just like your mini-chocolate chips.

CHAPTER 2

MOUNTAIN RANGES

If you hike up one of the higher peaks in the Appalachian Mountains, they can seem very high. But what you see now is a part of what the mountains once were. Geologists think the Appalachians could have been as high as the Himalayas—that's over four times as high as they are today! The Appalachians stretch from Maine to Alabama. Different sections formed at somewhat different times and in different ways, but together they form the backbone of the entire Eastern Coast region.

APPALACHIAN MOUNTAINS

There are numerous smaller mountain ranges that make up the Appalachians. These include the Blue Ridge Mountains in Virginia and North Carolina, and the Great Smoky Mountains of Tennessee and North Carolina. The Cumberland Mountains stretch through Tennessee, Kentucky, Virginia, and West Virginia, and the Allegheny Mountains are in Virginia, West Virginia, Maryland, and Pennsylvania. In the northern section are the Catskills of New York, the Berkshires of Massachusetts, the White Mountains of New Hampshire, and the Green Mountains of Vermont.

Appalachia is the southern part of the mountain chain in Georgia, Tennessee, Kentucky, Virginia, West Virginia, North Carolina, and Maryland.

Moving from east to west in the southern part of the Appalachians, you'll find the Piedmont area that is rolling hills, then the Blue Ridge Mountains, then the Valley and Ridge, which includes the Alleghenies and the Cumberland Mountains. Beyond is the Appalachian Plateau, which includes the Allegheny Plateau and the Cumberland Plateau.

The Appalachian Mountains are some of the oldest mountains on Earth. You'll find three major types of rocks in the Appalachians, depending on when and how they formed.

Did You Know?

Some mountain ranges, like the Catskill Mountains in New York, are actually plateaus that have eroded in places to make valleys. These dissected plateaus give the appearance of mountains.

21

The oldest rocks are usually metamorphic rocks, which were originally sedimentary or igneous rocks. They were buried over a billion years ago when continents crashed together. Old Rag Mountain in Virginia has beautiful examples of these old metamorphic rocks, with rounded peaks and lots of boulders. These are often called basement rocks because they're like the basement in a house. Just like the foundation of a house is poured first, these basement rocks formed first, and they hold everything else up.

Then volcanic rocks formed when the continents rifted apart. Lava bubbled out through rifts in the crust and cooled to form basalt. One lava flow cooled before the next eruption. As a result, the landscape often looks like a staircase built into steep cliffs. Later, when the basalt metamorphosed, the new minerals that formed had a greenish tint. These rocks are called greenstones because of their color.

Did You Know?

The Appalachian Mountains were a natural barrier for people traveling west. Daniel Boone was an explorer, fur trapper, and folk hero in the late 1700s. In 1775, Daniel Boone blazed a trail through the Cumberland Gap in the Appalachians in Virginia and Tennessee to Kentucky. At first it was just a path, but it was later widened to a track, called the Wilderness Road, that wagons could cross. The Wilderness Road allowed settlers to reach Kentucky and areas farther west.

Stony Man Peak in Shenandoah National Park in Virginia is a good example of a greenstone staircase.

Finally, the youngest rocks are sedimentary rocks that formed as a new ocean was forming across eastern North America. Calvary Rocks Peak in Virginia contains examples of these steep-sloped sedimentary rocks.

Although many rocks originally formed in different environments, the main event that actually pushed the rocks into mountains was the Appalachian Orogeny. As North America collided with Africa, the rocks were jammed together and pushed upward. Rocks folded and faulted fiercely. As rocks were buried, the pressure and increased heat changed them into different rocks, which is called metamorphism.

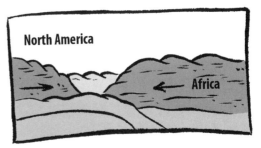

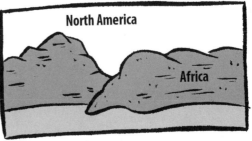

These metamorphosed rocks are often harder and less resistant to erosion.

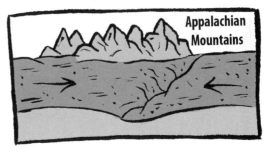

WEATHERING AND EROSION

The rocks we see today at the tops of the Appalachian Mountains were far beneath the surface of the earth when the mountains were much higher. These rocks were exposed as the mountains eroded. And they're still being eroded every day. How does this happen? Through a process called weathering and erosion.

Weathering is when rocks are broken down from large pieces into small pieces. This happens by physical processes or chemical processes. Erosion is when the smaller rock pieces are moved away. Once rocks are broken down, the smaller pieces are eroded away by moving water, glaciers, or gravity—either falling or slowly creeping downhill.

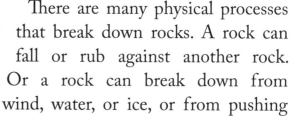

Mount Katahdin, Maine

Springer Mountain, Georgia

There are many physical processes that break down rocks. A rock can fall or rub against another rock. Or a rock can break down from wind, water, or ice, or from pushing by strong tree and plant roots. Chemical processes also break down rocks, such as when **acidic** water flows over a rock. Taste plain lemon juice and the acid in it will make your mouth pucker! All rainfall is naturally slightly acidic because **carbon dioxide** in the air reacts with water to form carbonic acid.

Did You Know?

The Appalachian Trail runs from Mount Katahdin in Maine to Springer Mountain in Georgia, and passes through 14 states. It is about 2,181 miles long (3,510 kilometers). Early Native Americans created sections of the trail. The official trail was established in 1937. A "through-hiker" is someone who hikes the whole trail in one season, usually from around March to October. Some sections are extremely steep, and hikers must hold on to trees and roots while climbing.

The drip-drop of rain or the slow movement of glaciers may not seem like enough to erode mountains 20,000 feet high (6,000 meters) down to less than 5,000 feet (1,500 meters), but that's exactly what has happened. Because in the Appalachians, there's been plenty of time—the last ingredient needed for erosion to occur!

HIGH MOUNTAINS

The highest "mountain" above sea level in each state of the region is listed below. You might notice that some states list a "hill" or "azimuth" or "high point" because they don't really have any mountains. There are five states in America that have a highest point that is less than 1,000 feet above sea level (305 meters), and all of them are in the Eastern Coast region.

Alabama	Cheaha Mountain	2,405 feet (733 meters)
Arkansas	Magazine Mountain	2,753 feet (840 meters)
Connecticut	Mt. Frissell—Slope	2,380 feet (725 meters)
Delaware	Ebright Azimuth	448 feet (137 meters)
Florida	Britton Hill	345 feet (105 meters)
Georgia	Brasstown Bald	4,784 feet (1458 meters)
Kentucky	Black Mountain	4,139 feet (1,262 meters)
Louisiana	Driskill Mountain	535 feet (163 meters)
Maine	Mt. Katahdin	5,267 feet (1,605 meters)
Maryland	Backbone Mountain	3,360 feet (1,024 meters)
Massachusetts	Mt. Greylock	3,487 feet (1,063 meters)
Mississippi	Woodall Mountain	806 feet (246 meters)
New Hampshire	Mt. Washington	6,288 feet (1,917 meters)
New Jersey	High Point	1,803 feet (550 meters)
New York	Mt. Marcy	5,344 feet (1,629 meters)
North Carolina	Mt. Mitchell	6,684 feet (2,037 meters)
Pennsylvania	Mt. Davis	3,213 feet (979 meters)
Rhode Island	Jerimoth Hill	812 feet (247 meters)
South Carolina	Sassafras Mountain	3,560 feet (1,085 meters)
Tennessee	Clingmans Dome	6,643 feet (2,025 meters)
Vermont	Mt. Mansfield	4,393 feet (1,339 meters)
Virginia	Mt. Rogers	5,729 feet (1,746 meters)
West Virginia	Spruce Knob	4,861 feet (1,482 meters)

GREAT SMOKY MOUNTAINS NATIONAL PARK

Great Smoky Mountains National Park, on the border between Tennessee and North Carolina, is America's most visited park. It contains very old mountains, with lots of metamorphic rocks. The Great Smokies contain many high mountains, with one stretch running for 36 miles (58 kilometers), all above 5,000 feet (1,500 meters). The highest peak is Clingmans Dome at 6,643 feet (2,000 meters)

WORDS TO KNOW

old-growth forest: a forest that is very old.

habitat: the natural area where a plant or animal lives.

biodiversity: the range of living things in an area.

species: a group of plants or animals that are related and look like each other.

organism: any living thing.

The park gets lots of rain, with about 55 inches per year in the valleys (140 centimeters) and 85 inches per year in the peaks (215 centimeters). This is more rain than anywhere else in the United States except the Pacific Northwest. With all that rain, plants thrive. Almost all of the park is forest, and one quarter of that is **old-growth forest**.

Because of changes in elevation, the Great Smokies contains lots of different **habitats**. This means that the park has an incredible **biodiversity**. Scientists have found many different plants and animals in the park:

- Over 17,000 **species** of **organisms**, and scientists think there may be as many as 80,000 more!

- Over 100 species of trees, which is more than there are in all of northern Europe.

- 1,600 species of flowering plants.

- 66 species of mammals, including gray and red foxes, coyotes, woodchucks, opossums, skunks, and bobcats. About 1,500 black bears live in the park.

- 200 species of birds and 50 species of fish.

- At least 30 species of salamanders.

Great Smoky Mountains National Park has 17 species of fireflies. A firefly is a type of beetle that flashes a light from its belly to attract a mate. If you live in the Eastern Coast region, you might see fireflies on warm summer evenings as flashes of light around your backyard.

One species of firefly in the Great Smokies is special. For about two weeks in June, synchronous fireflies flash in unison, all at the same time. Fireflies spend most of their life—up to two years—as **larvae**, before turning into an adult beetle. And then they only live as a beetle for 21 days, without eating the whole time!

Fireflies are bothered by bright lights. To watch fireflies, whether in the Smokies or in

WORDS TO KNOW

larvae: the wormlike stage of an insect's life.

Photurinae (Synchronous) Firefly

Phausis Reticulata (Blue Ghost)

your own backyard, cover your flashlight with red or blue cellophane. Only use your flashlight when you have to and point it at the ground. It's best not to catch fireflies so you don't accidentally hurt them.

Great Smoky Mountains National Park is called the "Salamander Capital of the World." Many salamanders don't breathe like you and I do. They breathe through their skin!

There are 24 species of salamanders that don't have lungs. They exchange oxygen through the walls of tiny blood vessels in their skin and linings of their mouths and throats. You can find lungless salamanders along streams, and under leaves and logs. Their skin is moist and they need to live in wet environments. The Great Smoky Mountains are the perfect place for these salamanders. The largest salamanders in the park are hellbenders, which grow as long as an average 15-month-old toddler is tall. That's 2 feet long (61 centimeters)!

MAKE YOUR OWN
FOLDED MOUNTAINS

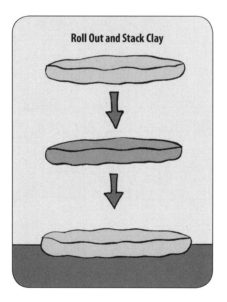

Roll Out and Stack Clay

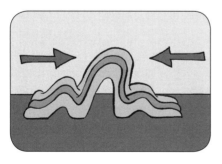

1 Roll out each color of clay into the size and shape of a very large pancake, about ¼ inch thick (½ centimeter). If you have enough clay, roll out extra layers. Stack the layers on top of each other, alternating colors.

2 Place your hands on the outside edges of the stack and gently push towards the middle. The clay should form into 2 or 3 folds. You may have to lift the middle up to help it form the folds. It's okay if the folds flop over a bit on their sides. This is like two tectonic plates colliding and forcing the crust to fold.

3 Rotate the folded clay 90 degrees. Repeat step 2 so that you are folding the folds. You will need to lift the middle to form the second fold. The clay should have rough dome shapes.

4 With the table knife, slice off the top ½ inch of the domes (1 centimeter). How do the layers of clay look? Try slicing vertically along one side of the dome. Then try slicing at an angle. This is like the erosion of rocks.

5 Try this again with new clay but experiment with different ways of folding the clay.

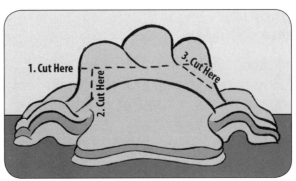

1. Cut Here
2. Cut Here
3. Cut Here

What's Happening?

When tectonic plates are on the move, rocks are often buried at great depths where it's much hotter. When forces act on these hot rocks, they can fold, just like your clay.

Often, rocks get pushed from different directions over time. When that happens, folds in the rocks can get re-folded, which is called superposed folding. This is what happened when you re-folded your clay. Then, when the rocks are later uplifted above the ground and eroded, the folds and rock layers can look different depending on where the erosion happened. The same thing happened when you cut the clay at different angles.

The Appalachian Mountains have undergone folding from forces in different directions. Many of these folds are exposed throughout the mountain chain in road cuts and other areas.

MAKE YOUR OWN
WEATHERING STATION

Have an adult supervise as glass can break.

1 Fill the glass jar with cold tap water all the way to the top. Tightly seal the jar with the lid. There should be no pockets of air.

2 Place the jar in the freezer bag and seal the bag. Place the jar and bag in the coldest part of the freezer overnight.

3 With an adult's help, carefully remove the bag and jar. What do you notice? Wrap the jar and bag in additional bags or paper and dispose of it in the trash.

SUPPLIES

- glass jar with lid (one that you don't mind breaking)
- cold tap water
- gallon-size plastic resealable freezer bag (3.8 liters)
- freezer

What's Happening?

If you freeze a liquid it turns into a solid. Usually, a solid takes up less space than a liquid. But water is unusual because it expands when it becomes a solid. When you froze the water in the jar, it expanded and exerted enough pressure on the glass to break it!

Frost action is one of the ways that weathering breaks rocks into pieces. First, water seeps into tiny cracks in rocks. When the temperature drops below freezing, the water freezes. Just like in your jar, the water expands as it freezes and exerts great pressure on the rock. This widens the small cracks. When the ice melts, water can seep even farther into the rock. When this happens over and over, even huge boulders can be reduced to pebbles over time.

CHAPTER 3

EARTHQUAKES AND RESOURCES

The forces of the earth can cause extreme hazards, or create great resources. Have you ever felt an earthquake? You don't hear about it often, but earthquakes periodically shake things up in many parts of the Eastern Region. There are also abundant resources, such as **coal**, **oil** and natural gas.

WORDS TO KNOW

coal: a dark brown or black rock formed from decayed plants. Coal is used as a fuel.

oil: a thick dark liquid that occurs naturally beneath the earth. Oil can be separated into many products, including gasoline and other fuels.

31

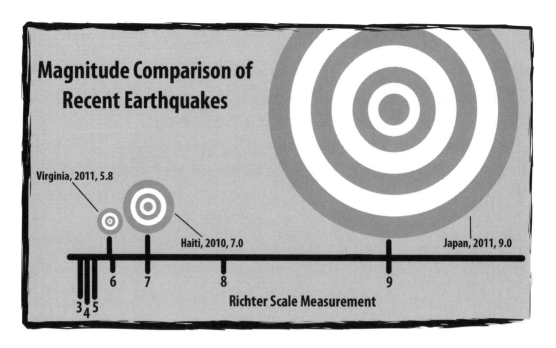

Magnitude Comparison of Recent Earthquakes

Virginia, 2011, 5.8

Haiti, 2010, 7.0

Japan, 2011, 9.0

3 4 5   6   7   8   9

Richter Scale Measurement

WORDS TO KNOW

Richter scale: a scale used to measure the strength of an earthquake.

seismic wave: a wave of energy generated from an earthquake. The wave travels through the earth.

EARTHQUAKES!

When stress builds up in rocks, they can suddenly lurch into a new position. That lurching is called an earthquake. Most earthquakes happen along faults, which are cracks in the outer layer of the earth called the lithosphere.

When an earthquake happens, it releases huge amounts of energy. Waves of energy travel out in all directions as **seismic waves**. It's a bit like when you toss a large rock into a pond. The ripples of water spread out in all directions.

Did You Know?

On March 11, 2011, an earthquake off the coast of Japan measured 9.0 on the **Richter scale**. It was the fourth-largest earthquake since the year 1900. But the earthquake in Haiti on January 12, 2010, was more devastating because it happened close to a large city where most of the buildings were poorly built and collapsed. It injured or killed hundreds of thousands of people.

HOW BIG IS THAT EARTHQUAKE?

Earthquakes are measured mainly by their magnitude. Magnitude is the strength of an earthquake and is recorded on the Richter scale. When the measurement increases by 1, the magnitude increases by 10. So an earthquake that measures 8.0 is 10 times as powerful as an earthquake that measures 7.0. Here are some typical effects that people might feel near the epicenter of earthquakes of various magnitudes. This is the point on the earth's surface directly above the location of the earthquake.

Magnitude on the Richter Scale	What it Feels Like	How Often They Occur in the World
Below 3.0	You usually can't feel it.	1,000 per day
3.0 to 3.9	You can feel a slight trembling, but there is no damage.	Over 100 per day
4.0 to 4.9	Tables and chairs rattle.	About 20 per day
5.0 to 6.9	Some damage to buildings, especially if they're poorly built.	About 3 per day
7.0 to 7.9	Serious damage to buildings, with some destroyed.	18 per year
8.0 to 8.9	Serious damage for several hundred miles.	1 per year
9.0 to 9.9	Devastating, affecting people for thousands of miles.	1 per 20 years
10.0 and up	Never recorded.	?

NEW MADRID SEISMIC ZONE

Do you know which state in the United States had the earthquake that affected the largest area in recorded history? Do you think of California? It's true that California has lots of earthquakes. But the earthquake that affected the largest area happened in New Madrid, Missouri. This is where the Eastern Coast region meets the Great Plains region in the center of the country.

The New Madrid Seismic Zone is a system of faults right in the middle of the North American Plate. The area is where Missouri, Kentucky, Arkansas, and Tennessee meet. There are several faults here about 150 miles long (241 kilometers), from Arkansas to southern Illinois. In 1811 and 1812, there were three huge earthquakes along these faults that measured between 7.5 and 8.0 on the Richter scale.

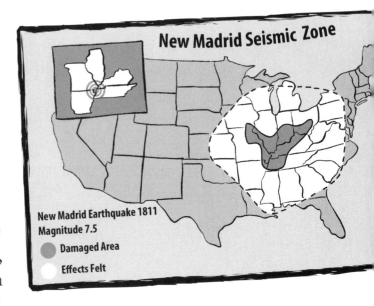

New Madrid Seismic Zone

New Madrid Earthquake 1811
Magnitude 7.5
● Damaged Area
○ Effects Felt

Since they happened before there were modern instruments to measure earthquakes, scientists have to estimate their strength based on newspaper reports and by looking at changes in the rocks.

34

These were the largest quakes east of the Rocky Mountains in recorded history. They were felt farther than much larger ones in Alaska because the older, colder rocks in the craton transmit seismic waves farther. People felt them from the Rocky Mountains to the Atlantic Ocean and from Canada to Mexico. Sidewalks buckled in Baltimore, Maryland, and chimneys fell down in Cincinnati, Ohio. Church bells rang in Boston, Massachusetts.

In Washington, D.C., President James Madison and his wife Dolly thought someone was robbing the White House. And the banks of the Mississippi River collapsed. In some places the earth tilted so much that the river ran backwards for a while!

Did You Know?

When the August 2011 earthquake hit in Virginia, people immediately began sending "tweets," the short electronic messages sent by the message service Twitter. The tweets actually reached people in New York City 40 seconds before the seismic waves did! The U.S. Geological Survey (USGS) monitors earthquakes using seismometers, which can take up to 20 minutes to generate an alert of an earthquake. The USGS is now experimenting with Twitter as a fast and cheaper way to track earthquakes.

WORDS TO KNOW

seismograph: an instrument that measures the intensity of a seismic wave.

Will another "Big One" happen? The only question is when. Each year there are about 500,000 earthquakes that are detectable by **seismographs**. About 100,000 can be felt by humans, but only 100 actually cause damage. In the area of New Madrid, there are earthquakes on most days, but you usually can't feel them.

EARTHQUAKES IN VIRGINIA?

On August 23, 2011, tourists stood 500 feet up on the observation deck of the Washington Monument (152 meters). As they looked out on the city of Washington, D.C., they felt the floor beneath them shake. Chips of stone started falling from the ceiling. It was an earthquake!

Effects of Quake Felt

Ottawa

Chicago

New York City

Washinton DC

Atlanta

Epicenter Magnitude: 5.8

Virginia Quake
August 23, 2011

Washington DC

Richmond

The Washington Monument shook violently and the visitors raced down the steps to the ground. Everyone got down safely, but the monument now has cracks on the outside and lots of damaged stone on the inside.

People on the East Coast aren't used to earthquakes. This one, centered in central Virginia, was 5.8 on the Richter scale, the largest in Virginia since 1897. Earthquakes in the central and eastern United States occur much less frequently than in the West, and they're usually of smaller magnitude.

The 2011 Virginia earthquake probably occurred along very old faults. The wave of energy traveled roughly along the Appalachian Mountains—northeast and southwest. It was felt as far away as New York City, Missouri, Canada, and Georgia.

BIG EARTHQUAKES IN THE PAST

A significant earthquake usually leaves a record of it in the rocks. Geologists can read that record, like you would read a book. They look closely at faults that have moved in the past 10,000 years. These are the best predictors of when and where earthquakes might occur in the future. What do geologists look for?

Paleoliquefaction is evidence of liquefaction that has occurred in the past. Liquefaction is when soil flows like a liquid, usually due to a large earthquake. The vibrations loosen the water-filled soil and break the grain-to-grain contact. Sometimes the sand "boils" when the liquefied sand bursts through surface clay and spills out. The New Madrid earthquakes produced lots of sand boils because, over millions of years, the Mississippi River has deposited huge amounts of sand covered over by clay. Scientists can see these circular areas of sand boils in pictures taken from the air.

Stalagmites are another clue. These are **cave** formations that scientists can study to date an earthquake. Stalagmites grow slowly when drips of water filled with minerals fall on the ground of a cave and slowly build up. If the earth moves in an earthquake, the source of the drip moves too. That makes the growth of the stalagmite shift, and you can see where it changes. Scientists cut paper-thin slices where the change happened and analyze the minerals to tell when the crystals formed. This is the date of the earthquake.

> ### WORDS TO KNOW
>
> **cave:** a natural underground opening connected to the surface, large enough for a person to enter.
>
> **fossil fuels:** oil, natural gas, and coal, which are natural fuels that formed long ago from the remains of living organisms.
>
> **natural gas:** a colorless, odorless gas used as a fuel.
>
> **fossil:** the remains or traces of ancient plants or animals.

Did You Know?

The USGS shows earthquakes in the United States for the last seven days on its web site: earthquake.usgs.gov/earthquakes. There are usually dots for earthquakes around the "boot heel" in the southeast corner of Missouri for the New Madrid Seismic Zone.

NATURAL RESOURCES

There are three major types of **fossil fuels**—coal, oil, and **natural gas**, and the Eastern Coast region has plenty of all three. They're called fossil fuels because just like **fossils**, they formed long, long ago from living organisms.

37

Formation of Fossil Fuels

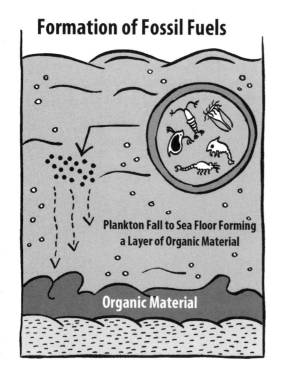

Plankton Fall to Sea Floor Forming a Layer of Organic Material

Organic Material

WORDS TO KNOW

organic material: matter that has come from organisms.

carbon: an element found in all living things.

mine: to dig something out of the ground.

Most fossil fuels formed hundreds of millions of years ago—even before the dinosaurs. Many areas were covered with swamps, huge trees, and other plants. There were also shallow inland seas with tiny floating sea creatures called plankton.

Coal, oil, and natural gas all form through a similar process. First, plants or plankton die and sink to the bottom of the swamp or ocean. Layers of this **organic material** build up and are covered by sediments. As more and more layers of sediments and organic material build up, heat and pressure turn the organic material into coal, oil, or natural gas. The difference is in the original material. Coal comes from trees or plants, and oil and gas are formed from plankton.

COAL

Coal is a black rock that is made mostly of **carbon**. It can be burned to produce heat and electricity. The first known use of coal was in China about 3,000 years ago.

Coal can be **mined** by sinking tunnels, known as shafts, deep underground. Elevators take coal miners to the bottom of the shafts to dig the coal. Coal is also mined in strip mines where the layers above the coal are stripped away by machines. Most of the mines in the East are underground mines reached by shafts, because the coal is deep beneath the surface.

A LOST TOWN

Centralia, Pennsylvania, is a town that was burned out of existence. The land beneath the town began burning in 1962, when a fire somehow started near an abandoned coal mine. Miners can never extract all of the coal from a coal mine, and some is always left behind. If that remaining coal catches on fire, it is difficult to put out because it's burning underground.

People in Centralia slowly became aware of the fire beneath their feet. In 1981, a **sinkhole** 4 feet wide and 150 feet deep opened in a backyard (just over 1 meter wide and 46 meters deep). A 12-year-old boy fell in. Luckily, his cousin came to his rescue. After 30 years of slow burning, the state claimed the town in 1992 and demolished any remaining buildings. A few years later, the United States Postal Service took away the town's postal zip code. The fire is still burning and scientists think it may burn for hundreds of years.

WORDS TO KNOW

sinkhole: a hole or depression in the land, normally caused by erosion in the underlying rock. Sinkholes can swallow cars or even homes.

Coal has been mined throughout the Appalachian Mountains since the 1700s. Today, coal is still mined in West Virginia, Kentucky, and Pennsylvania. At first, people used picks and shovels, but late in the 1800s, they started using machines to cut into the coal.

Although safety has improved, coal mining is still a dangerous job. People can be hurt or even die from explosions, cave-ins, or gas poisoning. In 1907, 3,200 workers died in coal mining accidents. Today, about 30 people die each year mining coal in the United States. There's still a lot to be done to keep workers safe.

Coal Mining Regions of the Eastern Coast

OIL AND NATURAL GAS

Oil is also called petroleum. This thick liquid is used as a fuel for heating, and to power factories and cars. Oil and natural gas are found in pockets between layers of rock. They are less dense than other materials, and slowly rise through rock layers until they reach a layer that traps the oil and gas. Oil was first pumped from a well in Titusville, Pennsylvania, on August 27, 1859.

Maybe your family uses natural gas to heat your home or your water. Natural gas is also burned to produce electricity, and used as a **raw material**. It is usually found near oil deposits and forms in a similar way to oil. It can also be found in layers of shale, which is a sedimentary rock. These shale layers formed more than 300 million years ago, when shallow seas covered much of the interior of North America. Organic matter was buried with fine sediments. The sediments turned into shale, and the organic matter became natural gas.

WORDS TO KNOW

raw material: a material that can be used to make a new or useful product.

technology: tools, methods, and systems used to solve a problem or do work.

horizontal drilling: drilling for oil or gas where the well is horizontal or close to horizontal.

hydraulic fracturing: a process where liquids are pumped down a well at high pressure to force the surrounding rock to fracture, or crack.

It used to be too difficult to extract natural gas from most shale. The layers of shale are deep beneath the surface, and the gas is tightly bound in the shale and doesn't release easily. But people have developed new **technologies** to extract the natural gas. Two things make this possible: **horizontal drilling** and **hydraulic fracturing**.

Drillers first drill vertically down to a little above where the shale layer is. Then the pipes slowly curve until they are horizontal and running through the shale layer. Tiny holes are in sections of the pipe. Using hydraulic fracturing, water is forced through the tiny holes at extremely high pressure—strong enough to fracture, or "frack" the surrounding rock for hundreds of feet. The cracks release the natural gas, which flows up the pipe to the surface. It is collected and transferred by pipeline to storage tanks until it is used.

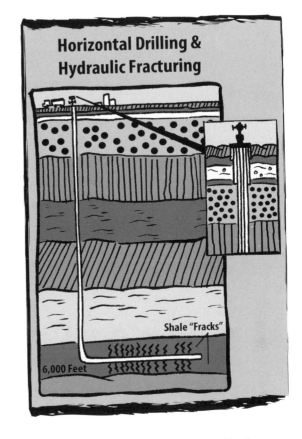

Horizontal Drilling & Hydraulic Fracturing

Shale "Fracks"

6,000 Feet

These "fracking" techniques have been used in a huge area called the Marcellus Shale. This is a layer of shale containing natural gas deep beneath the surface of the earth. It runs from New York through Pennsylvania, Ohio, West Virginia, Maryland, and Virginia, and is one of the largest areas of natural gas in the world. An even larger area of natural gas, the Utica Shale, is even deeper and extends a bit farther west into Ohio.

These two natural gas regions will make the United States one of the largest producers of natural gas in the world.

Did You Know?

The first natural gas well from shale in the United States was in Fredonia, New York, in 1821. Unlike more recent drilling in the Marcellus Shale, shale wells at that time were shallow.

OFFSHORE DRILLING

What do drillers face when they drill offshore, deep under the ocean? Almost-freezing water. Extreme pressure. Uncertain and sometimes dangerous weather. Drills can go 7,000 feet under water (2,100 meters), then deep into the earth. Most offshore oil wells are in shallower water (less than 500 feet deep or 150 meters), where the drilling platform can be attached to the ocean floor. But newer drilling techniques have allowed drilling in very deep water, where the giant drill rigs actually float on the water.

Oil wells have been drilled underwater since the late 1800s, but it's only since the 1930s that wells have been drilled in the Gulf of Mexico. There are wells off the shores of Florida, Alabama, Mississippi, Louisiana, and Texas.

DEEPWATER HORIZON OIL SPILL

On April 20, 2010 at 9:45 pm, a **geyser** of water erupted 240 feet (73 meters) into the air on the Deepwater Horizon drilling platform in the Gulf of Mexico. Then came an **eruption** of natural gas that caught fire, causing a series of explosions and a huge fireball.

Eleven people died in the explosion. The fire burned for 36 hours, then the entire rig sank. Oil from the well gushed deep underwater for three months. It was the largest offshore oil spill in the history of the United States.

Did You Know?

We put "gas" in our car to make it run, but that kind of gas is short for gasoline, and it's actually a liquid that comes from oil. Natural gas, like air, is a gas.

WORDS TO KNOW

geyser: a liquid shooting high into the air.

eruption: a violent explosion of gas, steam, or ash.

The Deepwater Horizon was an extremely deep well. It went through 4,132 feet of water (1,259 meters), then 35,050 feet of rock (10,683 meters).

42

When a pipe breaks off in very deep water, it's hard to stop the oil leak. There's a giant shut-off valve called a blowout preventer, which is supposed to stop the flow of oil and cap the well if there's a problem. For some reason, the blowout preventer didn't work on the Deepwater Horizon, and the oil gushed into the ocean.

It's very difficult to cap off a well if the blowout preventer doesn't work. And in extremely deep water, it's even harder. The pressure is so great at that depth that it would crush a human like crumpling paper. The temperatures are so cold that the water is almost freezing. And if that isn't enough, ocean currents can be powerful at the bottom of the ocean.

Tiny blobs of oil naturally seep into the ocean all the time. Normally, **microbes** and sunlight break it down. But microbes and sunlight can't keep up with all the oil from a spill, and it builds up. Because oil mostly floats on the surface of the ocean after a spill, it spreads out in a thin layer that is hard to clean up. And the oil is harmful to wildlife.

Oil Well

43

- Bird feathers get coated in oil, making it hard for them to float and stay warm.

- Sea turtles and marine mammals become coated with oil.

- Marine mammals sometimes swallow oil.

- Sea corals are coated with oil and die.

The company that owns Deepwater Horizon is working with scientists to clean up the mess, and to help protect and restore wildlife harmed by the spill. The warm waters of the Gulf help to break down the oil faster than if it had spilled in colder water. But the best solution is to prevent spills before they happen.

Some people think that drilling for oil in the ocean, especially in deep water, is too risky for humans and the environment. Many believe it should be banned. Others think that we need to keep drilling so we don't have to rely on other countries for oil. They think we need to figure out what went wrong and change how we operate to prevent spills. What do you think? How would you find out more to decide?

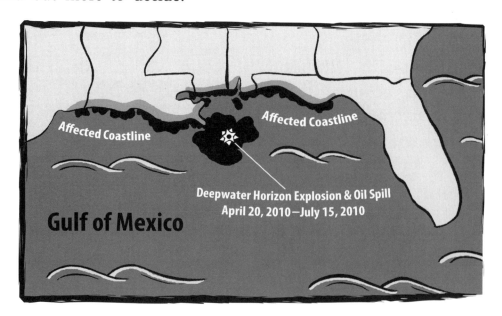

Affected Coastline

Affected Coastline

Deepwater Horizon Explosion & Oil Spill
April 20, 2010 – July 15, 2010

Gulf of Mexico

MAKE YOUR OWN
FRACKING HOSE

CAUTION: Have an adult help with the hammering.

1 Ask your parents if there is an unused garden hose you can use. You might also find one at a yard sale. It's fine if it leaks.

2 Find the end that attaches to the water spigot. A few feet from that end (about 1 meter), hammer the nail into the hose with an adult's help. Pull out the nail and move it about 2 inches away (5 centimeters). Make a hole about every 2 inches until you reach the end. Tightly screw the hose cap onto the end of the hose.

3 Attach the hose to the spigot. Turn the spigot on at full pressure. Where does the water go? Why do you think the water sprays up high instead of dribbling out of the holes?

4 You can reuse your hose as a soaker hose to steadily water garden plants. Bury the hose under soil or mulch next to plants, and turn the water on low. It will slowly water your plants.

SUPPLIES

- old, unused garden hose
- nail
- hammer
- cap for a garden hose
- outdoor water spigot

What's Happening?

Fracking works a lot like your hose, only at much higher pressures. Water is forced through holes in the drill pipes at extremely high pressure—enough to fracture, or "frack" the surrounding rock.

MAKE YOUR OWN
EARTHQUAKE WAVES

1 Grab the posterboard with both hands on one end. While standing, gently shake the posterboard. Does it move like a wave?

2 Make several creases in the posterboard. The creases should be in different directions—some parallel to the side you held, and some at a diagonal. Grab one end of the posterboard again and shake it. Does it move the same? How is it different?

SUPPLIES

- 1 sheet of posterboard 2 feet by 3 feet (about 60 by 90 centimeters)

What's Happening?

When you first shook the posterboard without creases, it was a bit like when earthquakes happen in the eastern United States. There aren't as many faults there, so seismic waves travel without being interrupted. When you shook the posterboard with creases, it was more like earthquakes in the western United States. There are many faults throughout the west, which interrupt the seismic waves. Also, rocks in the East are generally older and colder, which allows seismic waves to travel farther.

MAKE YOUR OWN
OIL SPILL

1 Fill the baking dish about 2 inches deep with water. Slowly pour 1 tablespoonful of oil on top of the water. What does the oil do?

SUPPLIES

- large, shallow baking dish
- water
- tablespoon
- olive oil
- clean craft feather
- wide bowl
- dish detergent

2 Holding the feather over the sink, gently pour water over the feather. Run your fingers through the feather. Do the individual branches separate and fluff as it begins to dry? Now swish the feather in the oil in the baking dish so that the feather is coated in oil. Do the individual branches separate and fluff now?

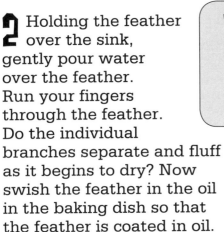

3 Fill the bowl with water. Pour one tablespoonful of detergent into the bowl and stir. Soak the feather in the mixture and gently work the detergent through the feather's branches with your fingers. As the feather dries, do the branches separate and fluff?

What's Happening?

Oil and water don't mix, and oil is less dense than water. So when oil is spilled in the ocean or rivers, the oil spreads out into a thin layer that coats the water. Wildlife, especially birds, can become coated in oil as they enter the water. It makes it difficult for birds to stay warm because oil-coated feathers don't insulate well. Scientists can sometimes help birds recover by carefully cleaning their feathers using detergent. And how do they clean up an oil spill? It's not easy. Try cleaning up your spill with different materials, such as sponges, paper towels, and nets.

CHAPTER 4

PLAINS

Plateaus and **plains** stretch for miles and miles east and west of the Appalachian Mountains. Sometimes rolling hills, and other times flat as a pancake, they make up most of the landscape and cover all or part of every state in the region. In some states, like Florida, Louisiana, Mississippi, Delaware, and Rhode Island, it's all you'll find. The plains give the region its beautiful beaches, **fertile** farmland, and incredible **bayous** and swamps.

WORDS TO KNOW

plain: a large area of flat land.

fertile: land that is good for growing plants.

bayou: a term used mainly in Mississippi and Louisiana for the swampy arm or slow-moving outlet of a lake.

COASTAL PLAINS, PIEDMONT, AND INTERIOR PLAINS

The coastal plain stretches from the eastern edge of New Jersey down the Atlantic coast, wrapping around Florida along the Gulf Coast. This area lies between the Appalachian Mountains and the ocean.

WORDS TO KNOW

bedrock: solid rock under loose material such as soil, sand, clay, or gravel.

floodplain: an area around a shallow winding river where the land is lower than other areas.

The **bedrock** on the coastal plain is mostly sedimentary rock that was deposited when the area was covered by the ocean. Later the region was uplifted, and it tilts slightly towards the sea. The coastal plain also has many sediments like gravel, sand, and clay on top of the bedrock.

Sediments have been stripped from the Appalachian Mountains and carried east by rivers.

In the past, the sea level was lower and the coastal plain also included areas that are now covered by seawater. An example of this is the Chesapeake Bay in Maryland, which used to be a **floodplain** of the Susquehanna River.

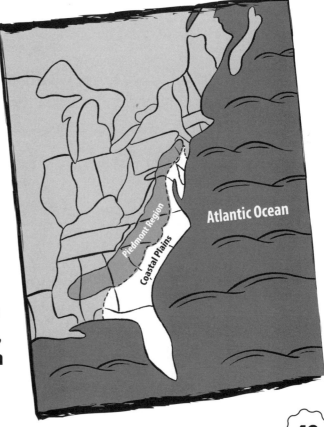

Piedmont Region

Coastal Plains

Atlantic Ocean

From New Jersey to central Alabama, the Piedmont region runs between the coastal plain and the Appalachian Mountains. The Piedmont is a plateau that formed along with the Appalachian Mountains as continents crashed together. The area has since eroded away to form rolling hills.

Millions of years ago, a shallow sea swept into the interior part of the country and covered the central part of the continent to the west of the Appalachian Mountains. The sea advanced and receded many times, which deposited flat layers of younger sedimentary rocks. These interior plains include the western sections of Tennessee and Kentucky, the northern section of Alabama, and the western section of New York.

Did You Know?

The highest point in Florida is only 345 feet high (105 meters), and its average elevation is only 98 feet above sea level (30 meters).

CAVES!

The Eastern Coast region has thousands of caves of all shapes and sizes. Some are just a shallow hollow in the earth, while others wind for tens or even hundreds of miles in total darkness.

WORDS TO KNOW

limestone: a type of rock that often forms from the shells of sea animals.

Some of the more famous caves in the region are Mammoth Cave in Kentucky, Luray Caverns in Virginia, and Russell Cave in Alabama.

Most of them are **limestone** caves. Layers of limestone were deposited when a shallow sea covered the interior of North America. Limestone was also deposited all along the coastal plain region when sea levels were higher.

Limestone is a type of rock that dissolves in slightly acidic water. It often has cracks in it, and rainwater seeps into these cracks. The acid in the rainwater slowly dissolves the rock, making the cracks wider. In some caves, a stream can travel through the limestone until it finds an outlet, eroding even more rock along the way. Eventually, part of the roof can collapse, which forms **caverns**.

Large areas of the Eastern Coast region have what is called a karst landscape. That is where the bedrock is limestone that has been dissolved, forming sinkholes, sinking streams, and caves. From an airplane, a karst landscape can look pockmarked. Nearly half of the coastal plain has this type of landscape.

CAVE FORMATIONS

Once caverns form, cave formations of all shapes and sizes can develop that look like teeth, columns, curtains, pearls, and beards! These cave formations are called **speleothems**. As rainwater seeps through limestone and dissolves it, the limestone doesn't disappear—it's just in the water. When water drips from the ceiling of a cave, a very small bit of limestone is left behind. Drop by drop, huge speleothems form. Maybe you've seen pictures of stalactites and stalagmites.

The kind of speleothem formed depends mainly on whether the water drips, trickles, or seeps into the cave. Here are some formations you might find in caves:

- **Stalactites** grow where water drips from the ceiling.

- **Stalagmites** grow where water drips onto the floor.

- **Draperies** grow where water runs down a slanted ceiling or wall.

- **Columns** are where a stalactite and stalagmite meet.

- **Soda straws** are hollow tubes that grow where water seeps through the ceiling. They can turn into a stalactite if the hole at the bottom gets blocked.

- **Pearls** grow in pools of calcite-rich water like an oyster pearl. They grow layer upon layer around a grain of sand.

- **Flowstone** grows where water flows over walls or floors.

- **Beards** are clumps of delicate, thin threads that grow from water containing a dissolved mineral called gypsum.

- **Popcorn** formations are clusters that look like popcorn or grapes. They are found on ceilings, floors, and walls.

SINKHOLES!

Sinkholes are openings in the ground that appear where the rock underneath has dissolved. This usually happens in a karst landscape because the limestone has dissolved from slightly acidic water. Sinkholes can slowly sink, or open up all at once. When that happens, a sinkhole can swallow entire houses! After it forms, a sinkhole might swallow a river, fill with water and become a lake, or open an entrance to a cave. The Eastern Coast region has some amazing sinkholes!

• The "December Giant" sinkhole opened on December 2, 1972 in Shelby County, Alabama. Hundreds of tons of rock and dirt collapsed to make a hole 350 feet wide (107 meters), 450 feet long (137 meters), and 150 feet deep (46 meters). It's one of the biggest sinkholes in America.

• Kingsley Lake is an almost circular lake in north-central Florida that's 90 feet deep (27 meters). It probably formed when the limestone underneath dissolved and created a sinkhole.

• Cass Cave in West Virginia has a pit 140 feet deep (43 meters), which swallows a stream.

• A sinkhole opened in Winter Park, Florida, in 1981. It is 320 feet wide and 90 feet deep (98 meters wide and 27 meters deep), and swallowed a car dealership, a public pool, and a two-story house when it opened!

MAMMOTH CAVE

Mammoth Cave in Kentucky is the world's longest known cave system. More than 392 miles of the cave have been explored (631 kilometers), and every year more passages are found and mapped. The passages are interconnected and complex. If you want to visit the cave's most interesting places, head to Frozen Niagara, Grand Avenue, and Fat Man's Misery. Until the 1990s, you could take a boat ride on an underground river. There's even a hotel inside the cave that you can stay in!

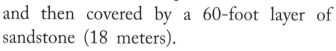

Mammoth Cave had its beginning about 350 million years ago, when a shallow, inland, saltwater sea covered the interior of North America. A 700-foot layer of limestone was deposited (213 meters) and then covered by a 60-foot layer of sandstone (18 meters).

WORDS TO KNOW

adapt: changes a plant or animal makes to survive.

albino: a human, animal, or plant that is very pale and does not have the usual amount of skin, eye, and hair color.

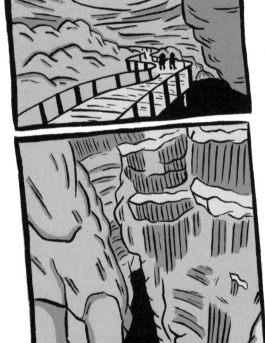

Later, the sandstone was eroded away. By 10 million years ago there were enough cracks and holes that rainwater began seeping into the limestone below. The slightly acidic rainwater slowly carved out caves and passages. In the lower layers, the cave is still forming today.

Mammoth Cave has stalagmites and stalactites, draperies, and soda straws. Mixed in with the limestone is another mineral, called gypsum. The seeping rainwater picks up bits of gypsum, which it then deposits in the caves. Gypsum formations, called gypsum flowers, are very delicate, and they form only in upper, dry parts of the cave because gypsum dissolves so easily in water.

Mammoth Cave has an amazing array of unusual animals. Living in total darkness means that animals have to **adapt** in interesting ways. There are 12 different species that are **albino** and don't have eyes, because they live in the pitch black of the deep caves. These include fish, crayfish, shrimp, and beetles.

EXPLORATION OF MAMMOTH

People first explored Mammoth Cave at least 4,000 years ago. There's even evidence that Native Americans mined the cave for crystals and gypsum. The cave was re-discovered in 1797, and has been open for tours since 1816.

One of the great explorers of Mammoth Cave was Steven Bishop, a young **slave** who first saw Mammoth in 1838. Using just a lantern and rope, he explored deep caverns and discovered rivers and **chasms**. He taught himself to read so he could study books about caves. Bishop named many of the rivers and formations in Mammoth, and made a map of it in 1842 that was used for 40 years. Some people believe that Bishop used Mammoth Cave as a place to hide runaway slaves as they escaped north.

WORDS TO KNOW

slave: a person owned by another person and forced to work without pay, against their will.

chasm: a deep crack or hole.

Three endangered species live in Mammoth Cave, including the Indiana bat, the Gray bat, and the cave shrimp. There are also many fossils in the limestone, even fossilized teeth from sharks!

GLACIERS

Most of the northern areas of the Eastern Coast have been transformed by the action of glaciers. How do glaciers form? How did glaciers come so far south, and why aren't they here now? When more snow falls than melts each year, it accumulates and eventually forms a glacier.

There are two main types of glaciers: alpine and continental. Alpine glaciers are formed in valleys high in the mountains where temperatures are colder. Continental glaciers are huge ice sheets that completely cover the land of a major part of a continent. Today, there are continental glaciers on Greenland and Antarctica. But in the past, continental glaciers covered much of northern North America and northern Europe and Asia.

WORDS TO KNOW

Ice Age: a period of time when large ice sheets cover large areas of land. It particularly refers to the most recent series of glaciations during the Pleistocene. An ice age can include shorter periods when glaciers retreat, as well as periods when the glaciers grow.

glaciation: when a large part of the earth is covered in ice.

glacial period: a period of time within an ice age when a large part of the earth's surface is covered with ice.

interglacial period: a period within an ice age that is somewhat warmer and glaciers retreat.

ICE AGE!

Earth's climate goes through natural variations in temperature over time. This is due to the earth's distance from the sun, how Earth turns on its axis, and where the continents are.

In the last 2.5 million years, until about 10,000 years ago, there have been at least 11 major cycles of cooling and warming. This entire time is called the Pleistocene, or sometimes just the **Ice Age**. During the cold periods, **glaciation** occurred as temperatures dropped over many, many years and glaciers expanded. These are called **glacial periods**. When the climate warmed and temperatures rose, called **interglacial periods**, the glaciers shrank.

During the glacial periods of the Ice Age, about 30 percent of the land on Earth was covered in ice up to 2 miles thick (3 kilometers).

The most recent glaciation lasted until about 10,000 years ago. Ice covered the New England states of Maine, New Hampshire, Vermont, Massachusetts, Connecticut, and Rhode Island, as well as most of New York and northern sections of New Jersey and Pennsylvania.

No one knows whether the Ice Age is over or still going on. Interglacial periods last about 10,000 to 12,000 years, and we've been in an interglacial period for about that long. Human effects on the climate could possibly delay the start of another glacial period.

GLACIAL LANDFORMS

Glaciers erode the land and reshape it. When glaciers move, their great weight cracks and crushes the rock beneath. The glacier plucks up chunks of rock and carries them along. The chunks can vary in size from fine sediment called rock flour to house-sized boulders. They are frozen into the ice and, as they move, the rock chunks grind and polish the bedrock underneath—a bit like sandpaper.

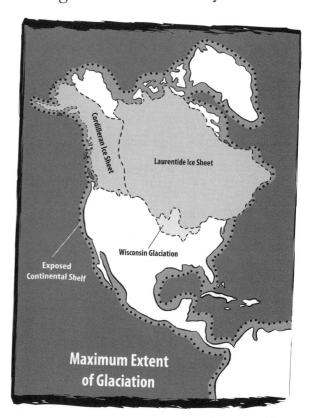

Cordilleran Ice Sheet

Laurentide Ice Sheet

Wisconsin Glaciation

Exposed Continental Shelf

Maximum Extent of Glaciation

When the glacier melts, it deposits this material into various landforms.

Many of these effects of glaciers might be hard to recognize because the landforms are covered over by grasslands, forests, and fields. But look beyond the vegetation and you might see some clues that a glacier has been around.

57

Scratches and grooves in the bedrock are deep parallel scratches where the glacier scraped over ground carrying broken rock. Cadillac Mountain on Mount Desert Island was probably the first surface to emerge when the glacier that once covered the whole state of Maine melted. There are grooves on the bedrock in north-south parallel lines because the glacier moved and shaped the land from north to south.

If you ever get a chance to look at Cadillac Mountain, you'll see that it's shaped like a cat. It has gently sloping north and south sides, and steep east and west sides.

Glacial polish is like polishing brass with cleaner that has a bit of grit in it. Glaciers with rock flour polish the underlying bedrock. The rock has a smooth surface, almost like glass.

Till is a random mixture of clay, rocks, and gravel, which is carried along by a glacier and then deposited as the ice melts.

Moraines are deposits of till that form on the sides and front of glaciers. As the glacier melts, the till is dropped out into mounds and ridges. Terminal moraines trace the farthest edge of a glacier. On Long Island in New York, there are many terminal moraines.

Eskers occur when a glacier has a river flowing underneath it. That river deposits material just like regular rivers do. When the entire glacier melts, the deposited material forms a meandering ridge of till called an esker.

Did You Know?

Twice in the long-ago past—710 and 635 million years ago—scientists believe Earth was covered in ice sheets, even at the equator! Scientists call this the Snowball Earth Theory. Even during this deep freeze, life survived in the form of tiny, single-celled microbes.

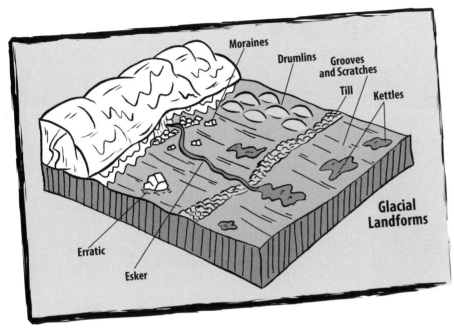

Moraines
Drumlins
Grooves
and Scratches
Till
Kettles
Glacial
Landforms
Erratic
Esker

Great Esker Park in Weymouth, Massachusetts, is 90 feet high and is the highest esker in North America (27 meters).

Erratics are rocks that have been carried by a glacier from another location. They can be as small as a pebble or as large as a house. Scientists try to determine where erratics came from to help them map the flow directions of the glacier. On a visit to Central Park in New York City, you can see many huge erratics, as well as grooves and gouges left by glaciers on the bedrock.

Did You Know?

Glaciers often have a bluish or greenish tint because most of the air has been squeezed out.

Drumlins are smooth, teardrop-shaped mounds that were molded by a glacier. These often occur in groups and from above can look like a pod of whales swimming.

Kettles are bowl-shaped depressions that form when a block of ice is separated from the glacier and covered by till. When the ice later melts, the till collapses into a bowl shape. Spruce Hole Bog in Durham, New Hampshire is a kettle hole that has filled with water to form a bog.

MAKE YOUR OWN
CAVERN

SUPPLIES

- box of sugar cubes
- large glass jar
- tweezers
- modeling clay
- toothpick
- water
- cup or spray bottle
- food coloring

1 Use tweezers to arrange the sugar cubes in stacks of different heights in the jar. Make sure to completely line the inside edge of the jar with sugar cubes.

2 Completely cover the opening of the jar with a layer of clay at least ⅛ inch thick (⅓ centimeter). Make sure there aren't any gaps.

Clay

Sugar

3 Use the toothpick to poke holes in the clay. Make sure the holes reach to the sugar cubes. Try poking a few holes on one side of the jar, and many holes on the other side.

4 Put water in a cup or spray bottle, and add food coloring. Spray, or slowly pour, a few spoonfuls of water over the top of the clay.

5 As the water seeps through the holes, look at the sugar cubes that are touching the sides of the jar. What's happening? Let the experiment sit for a while, then add more water. Are passageways forming?

Did You Know?

Like most caves, Mammoth Cave has temperatures that remain steady at 54 degrees Fahrenheit all year round (12 degrees Celsius).

What's Happening?

The sugar cubes represent the limestone in Mammoth Cave. The spaces between are the cracks and spaces in the limestone, and the clay represents the overlying sandstone. Like limestone, the sugar dissolves in water, which can leave behind open spaces, or caverns.

MAKE YOUR OWN KETTLES

1 Cut the milk cartons in half. Rinse out the bottom halves and throw away the tops or keep them to use as garden scoopers.

2 Fill the bottom of one of the cartons with a single layer of gravel. Fill both cartons almost to the top with water and place them in the freezer overnight.

SUPPLIES

- 2 half-gallon paperboard milk cartons (1.89 liters)
- scissors
- gravel
- water
- freezer
- clay
- towel

1. Gravel

MILK

2. Water

MILK

3 Take the cartons out of the freezer and cut the carton away. If you have trouble releasing the carton, run it under warm water for a minute. The pieces of gravel should be sticking out slightly from the ice. If they aren't, run the ice under warm water for a minute to expose the gravel.

4 Roll the clay into a flat rectangle. Use the towel to hold the chunk of ice without the gravel and place the ice at one end of the clay. Drag the ice along the clay with a slight downward pressure. Are there marks on the clay? Then repeat using the ice that contains gravel. Are there marks on the clay now?

What's Happening?

Glaciers contain sediments of all sizes, from fine-grained silt to huge boulders. As the glacier moves over the ground underneath, the sediment scours away soil and sand. Because of the great weight of the overlying ice, larger pieces of sediment can scrape grooves into rocks underneath, just as your gravel-filled ice did with the clay.

CHAPTER 5

CLIMATE

From the tip of Maine to the very end of Florida, the Eastern Coast has some of the most diverse weather in America. If you travel from north to south, you'll cross four climate zones! You could pass through huge **Nor'easters** dumping heavy snowfall across the Mid-Atlantic and New England states in the winter, before arriving at the **subtropical** and even **tropical** beaches of the south. And watch out for scorching heat waves and **hurricanes** up and down the coast in the summer!

WORDS TO KNOW

Nor'easter: a storm blowing from the northeast, usually along the northeastern coast of the United States. It often brings high winds and cold temperatures.

subtropical: an area close to the tropics where the weather is warm.

tropical: a hot climate, usually near the equator.

hurricane: a severe tropical storm with winds greater than 74 miles per hour.

latitude: the lines that run west and east on the globe parallel to the equator. Latitudes vary from zero degrees at the equator to 90 degrees at the North and South Poles.

equator: an imaginary line around the earth, halfway between the North and South Poles.

WHAT MAKES THE WEATHER?

All the weather on the planet starts out with the sun. The sun's energy is what heats the earth and changes the temperature of a certain area. But why isn't it always warm when the sun shines in the winter? And why is Florida warmer than Maine when they both receive sunlight?

The answer has to do with something called **latitude**. Lines of latitude are imaginary lines "drawn" around the earth parallel to the **equator**. If you live in a latitude that is on or close to the equator, the sun's rays hit your location on Earth directly for the longest amount of time.

As you move into areas of latitude farther north or south from the equator, sunlight hits at more of an angle. This spreads out the energy from the sun so the earth doesn't heat up as much in these areas. The angle of sunlight is also why you feel more heat from the sun at noon, when the sun is directly overhead, than you do in the late afternoon.

The Eastern Coast region stretches all the way from the north to the south of the United Sates. The more southern areas are at a latitude closer to the equator and receive more energy from the sun than the northern areas. For this reason, the average temperature in July in Florida is 92 degrees Fahrenheit (33 degrees Celsius), while the average in Maine is 73 degrees Fahrenheit (23 degrees Celsius).

What else affects the Eastern Coast climate? The oceans. Being next to the Atlantic Ocean and the Gulf of Mexico means that the temperatures near the coast are much less extreme than they are in the middle of the country. Huge bodies of water like the ocean heat up and cool down more slowly than air or land, so oceans help keep the temperature milder.

Altitude can also make a big difference in climate. As you get higher up, the temperature tends to drop. As you climb a mountain, you can expect the air temperature to fall by an average of 3.6 degrees Fahrenheit every 1,000 feet you climb (2 degrees Celsius per 305 meters). This is because the atmosphere acts like a blanket to keep heat in. At higher altitudes, there aren't as many air molecules, so the "blanket" isn't as thick and heat escapes. In the Appalachian Mountains, temperatures are cooler than at lower altitudes and a similar latitude.

WORDS TO KNOW

altitude: the elevation, or height above sea level.

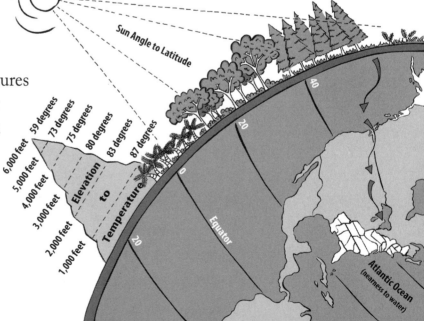

WEATHER AND CLIMATE: WHAT'S THE DIFFERENCE?

People often get weather and climate confused. Weather is what happens in the atmosphere related to temperature, **precipitation**, winds, and clouds. Climate is the average weather of a place over a long period of time.

Gatlinburg, Tennessee, is located only 25 miles away from Clingmans Dome (40 kilometers), the highest point on the Appalachian Trail. In January, when the average temperature in Gatlinburg is 51 degrees Fahrenheit (10.5 degrees Celsius), it's only 35 degrees Fahrenheit on Clingmans Dome (1.7 degrees Celsius).

HURRICANE!

Hurricanes are huge spinning storms that rotate around a point of **low pressure**. They form over tropical oceans and carry torrential rain and high winds. When they strike land, hurricanes can be deadly. Six out of the ten most expensive disasters to clean up in the United States have been from hurricanes. How do they start? Why are they so destructive? Let's find out!

WORDS TO KNOW

precipitation: rain, snow, or any form of water falling to Earth.

low pressure: a pocket of air in the atmosphere that is not pushing down strongly toward Earth.

tropical storm: a revolving storm that forms in the tropics.

evaporate: when a liquid heats up and changes into a gas.

water vapor: water as a gas, like steam or mist.

Hurricanes are born as **tropical storms** over warm waters close to the equator. The water needs to be at least 80 degrees Fahrenheit (26.5 degrees Celsius), but the air above needs to be cooler so thunderstorms can form. In the late summer months, the water near the equator warms up enough to **evaporate**. The **water vapor** rises up, creating large clouds full of moisture.

1.

**Warm Water Vapor Rises,
Creating Storm Clouds**

2.

**Surrounding Air is Pulled in
to Replace Rising Air and Moisture**

3.

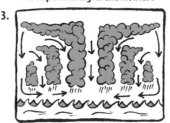

**This Cycle Continues, Producing Powerful Winds
Spinning the Clouds Into a Tropical Storm**

Life of a Hurricane

4.

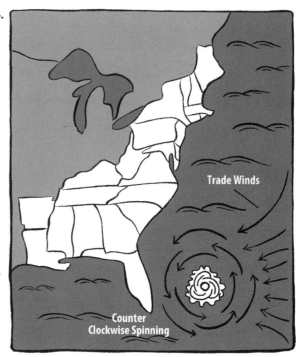

Trade Winds

Counter
Clockwise Spinning

**A Hurricane is Formed when High Winds Reach 75 MPH
and Spin the Storm Counter clockwise**

As the air and water vapor rise, air from surrounding areas swirls in to replace it. That air is warmed when it comes into contact with the ocean and it too rises up. This cycle continues, with more and more water vapor sucked up into the clouds. Powerful winds spin the clouds faster and faster into a tropical storm.

Most tropical storms sweep around the ocean for a day or two before dying out, but a few move on to bigger and more destructive things. Winds can push the storm westward across the Atlantic Ocean. That's when the storm does what it does best: slurp up more water vapor and grow bigger and faster and fiercer.

Did You Know?

The hurricane season lasts from June to November 30. The peak months are August and September.

When the wind in a tropical storm averages more than 75 miles per hour (120 kilometers per hour) and spins in a counterclockwise direction, it's a hurricane.

Hurricanes created in the Atlantic Ocean move west in the direction of North America. This is because they are pushed west by the **trade winds** across the **Northern Hemisphere**. Eventually, if it survives long enough, a hurricane will be blown into land, where it move all the way up the East Coast of the United States.

When a hurricane travels over land or over cold water, it loses energy. That's because a hurricane's tremendous energy comes from the heat of warm, tropical water. When you take away that energy source, the hurricane eventually dies out. But before it's over, the hurricane's heavy rains, strong winds, and large waves can do a lot of damage to trees, beaches, powerlines, buildings, and cars in coastal areas.

WORDS TO KNOW

trade winds: steady winds that blow from east to west in a belt between 30 degrees latitude above the equator to 30 degrees latitude below the equator.

Northern Hemisphere: the half of the earth north of the equator. The southern half is called the Southern Hemisphere.

WHAT'S IN A HURRICANE?

Maybe you've seen a picture of a hurricane from above, on the news. It looks a bit like a Frisbee. As hurricanes spin counterclockwise, they collect clouds that form in a huge circle. The very center of a hurricane is called the eye. All of the winds and clouds revolve around the eye. As air rises off the ocean and brings in water vapor and creates winds, the eye's open space forms where there are no clouds and the air is very calm.

Even though the eye is peaceful compared to the rest of the storm, the most dangerous part of a hurricane is right next to it. The eyewall is the area of clouds surrounding the eye, and the strongest winds and the most rain can be found there. The eyewall itself can be between 30 and 50 miles wide (48 to 80 kilometers).

Did You Know?

Hurricanes are huge heat engines, releasing energy through the formation of rain and the energy of the wind. The average hurricane releases 200 times as much energy in a day as the energy produced by all the electric power plants in the world. That's as much energy as about 10,000 nuclear bombs!

THE LARGEST STORMS ON EARTH

Hurricanes are the largest storms on Earth. Just how big? They can be 300 to 600 miles wide (483 to 965 kilometers) and about 10 miles high (16 kilometers). Sustained winds up to 155 miles per hour (250 kilometers per hour) can cover a large area, but winds can gust up to 225 miles per hour (360 kilometers per hour).

STORM SURGE!

Storm surge is the rise in the level of water caused by a storm. This becomes a big problem for people living on the coasts when a hurricane hits land. A storm surge isn't just a high wave—it's a wall of water that can overwhelm a coastal area. Storm surge as tall as 25 feet (7½ meters) is even taller than a house! Across the East Coast there are hundreds of towns and cities along the water. Storm surge floods streets, sweeping away cars and destroying buildings. In addition, storm surge sends waves much farther inland than usual. The frequent, high waves from hurricanes can batter buildings with great force.

Storm surge can be up to 25 feet high (8 meters). On top of the water moving in from the ocean, the giant clouds in a hurricane dump huge amounts of rain. Hurricanes can drop as much as 5 to 15 inches of rain in one hour (13 to 38 centimeters).

Even though a hurricane slows down and loses energy when it hits land, clouds carrying very heavy rains can drift miles and miles past the coast into the inland sections of the Eastern Coast region. In August 2011, Hurricane *Irene* caused the greatest damage in eastern New York state and Vermont. Heavy rain caused dramatic flooding, washing out bridges and roads.

HURRICANE KATRINA

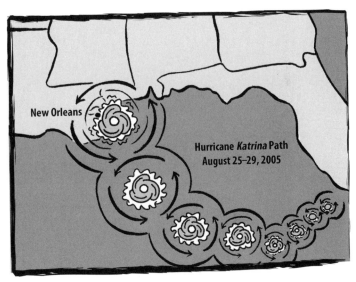

New Orleans

Hurricane *Katrina* Path
August 25–29, 2005

On August 29, 2005, the most destructive hurricane ever to strike the United States made landfall in Louisiana. Hurricane *Katrina* affected millions of people on the Gulf Coast. The storm surge in Louisiana, Mississippi, and Alabama was as high as 28 feet (8½ meters). Hurricane *Katrina* caused about $125 billion in damage, making it the costliest storm ever to hit the United States.

Interestingly, *Katrina* wasn't the most powerful hurricane ever to hit the United States. What made it so terrible? The geography of the area that Hurricane *Katrina* hit was a major factor in the severity of the storm. Normally, land gradually rises away from the ocean and is above sea level. But in New Orleans, Louisiana, sections of the city are 6 or 7 feet below sea level (about 2 meters).

Did You Know?

A storm with winds greater than 74 miles per hour (119 kilometers per hour) that occurs in the Atlantic Ocean, the Gulf of Mexico, or the eastern Pacific Ocean is called a hurricane. But in the western Pacific Ocean, East Asia, and Australia it's called a typhoon, and in the Indian Ocean it's called a cyclone.

New Orleans isn't directly on the ocean, but it sits right in between the Mississippi River and Lake Pontchartrain. To stop either of these bodies of water from flooding the city, huge levees surround it. A levee is a large wall made of concrete and steel built to hold water back.

As strong as they were, the levees in New Orleans were no match for the powerful storm surge from *Katrina*. They collapsed as soon as the storm hit. As a result, 80 percent of the city was covered in water, and almost all of the roads in and out of New Orleans were destroyed. Parts of the city were under 20 feet of water (6 meters)!

WINTER STORMS

Have you ever heard someone say that a storm front is coming into the area? Large areas of air are called air masses. When a warm, moist air mass collides with a cold, dry air mass, the area where they meet is called a front. Storms often occur along fronts because the air is unstable.

In the winter, strong storms can form when warm, moist air from the Gulf of Mexico rises over cold, dry air from Canada. When these two air masses meet, look out for intense snowstorms called **blizzards**! These storms often form near the Great Lakes because wind picks up moisture as it blows over the water, and then dumps it out as snow when it passes over land.

A Nor'easter is an intense storm that can occur in the eastern United States during the winter months. It's a lot like a hurricane. This low-pressure system rotates counterclockwise, and gets its initial energy from warmer water to the south. The storm travels to the northeast from the south, and the winds that drive it come from the northeast.

Nor'easters form when a storm coming from the south meets cold, Arctic air. The result can be high winds and snow so heavy you can barely see!

WORLD'S WORST WEATHER

Mt. Washington in the White Mountains in New Hampshire is known as the "Home of the World's Worst Weather." Three different storm tracks come together here, and the way the mountains are oriented from north to south causes the wind to blow even harder. Just how bad is it? In 1934, winds of 231 miles per hour were recorded (372 kilometers per hour). Mt. Washington receives annual snowfall of 256 inches (650 centimeters) and winds stronger than hurricane force for 104 days each year. Outside of Antarctica, it is one of the toughest places on Earth to live. But some scientists do exactly that: they take turns living and working in a weather station at the summit all year long to study the fascinating weather and climate on top of the mountain.

MAKE YOUR OWN
HURRICANE

1 Fill the bowl or sink to a couple of inches below the rim.

2 Use the spoon to stir the water in a circular, counterclockwise motion until the water is moving very fast. Drop a small amount of pepper into the water at the center of the bowl, some more pepper near the outside of the bowl, and some more about an inch from the center of the bowl. Watch how fast the pepper moves and where it goes.

3 If you like, stir the water again, and drop a few drops of food coloring near the outside of the bowl, at the center of the bowl, and about an inch from the center. Watch how the food coloring moves in the water.

SUPPLIES

- large bowl or sink
- water
- large spoon
- black pepper
- food coloring

74

What's Happening?

The center of your bowl is like the eye of a hurricane. The pepper and food coloring don't move very fast there. But the pepper and food coloring that you dropped an inch from the center move much faster than near the outside because this area is like the eyewall in a hurricane. You may notice the pepper and food coloring in the center getting "caught" by the swirling water around it and drawn outward. That's because the eye of your hurricane is very small, so the pepper and food coloring only stay in the eye for just a few seconds before they're swept outward. But the eye of a real hurricane is at least 5 miles wide, so there's plenty of room for a calm area.

HURRICANES' NAMES

Hurricanes have been given names of people for hundreds of years. In the West Indies, in the Caribbean Sea, people used to name hurricanes after saints. The practice of naming hurricanes became widespread during World War II. In 1953, female names in alphabetical order were used to officially name hurricanes. From 1979 on, six different lists of male and female names have been used in rotation for Atlantic Ocean hurricanes. So the list that was used in 2011 will be used again in 2017. If a storm is extremely deadly or costly, then the name is "retired" and not used again.

Did You Know?

The word hurricane comes from the Spanish word huracan, which comes from the Mayan word Hunraken. This was the name of their god of storms.

MAKE YOUR OWN
PRESSURE DIFFERENCES

CAUTION: This project involves matches, so have an adult help.

SUPPLIES

- hard boiled egg, peeled
- clear glass or heavy plastic bottle with neck slightly smaller than the egg
- piece of paper
- matches

1 Check to make sure the opening in the bottle is slightly smaller than the egg. Large juice or sports drink bottles often work well.

2 Scrunch up the paper and drop it into the bottle. Ask an adult to light the match and drop it into the bottle. Immediately place the egg on top of the bottle opening with the narrow side down.

What's Happening?

As the flame burns, it heats the air. Hot air takes up more space than cold air. You may have noticed the egg jumping on top of the bottle, letting the hot air out of the bottle. As the flame goes out, the air cools and takes up less space, lowering the air pressure inside the bottle. The higher air pressure outside pushes the egg into the bottle. A hurricane forms because of differences in air pressure. Close to the equator, the sun heats the air close to the surface of the water, and it rises. This creates low pressure near the surface of the ocean—just like the inside of your bottle. As a hurricane forms, air from surrounding areas is sucked into the low-pressure area, like the egg was sucked into the bottle.

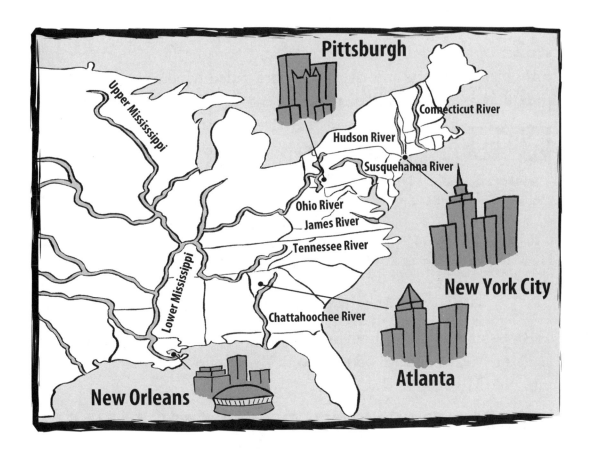

CHAPTER 6

RIVERS

ook on any map that shows rivers and cities. Do you notice anything? Most major cities are located along rivers, and it's not a coincidence. Plants, animals, and people all live near rivers. These bodies of water provide us with water, food, transportation, and recreation. The Eastern Coast gets plenty of rain and snow, which means it also has plenty of rivers. Rivers connect the landscape.

The water in rivers comes from precipitation that flows over the surface of the land. Smaller creeks and streams flow together and form bigger streams and rivers. They are called tributaries of the river they flow into. The land that drains into a river is the **watershed**

WORDS TO KNOW

watershed: the land area that drains into a river or stream.

crop: a plant grown for food and other uses.

of that river. A watershed is like a large bathtub. The sides of the bathtub are ridges or high elevation points. The drain is the river at the bottom. In a real bathtub, any drop of water that falls into it eventually flows to the drain. On land, the water flows to the river.

All rivers flow into an ocean somewhere.

Rivers in the East drain into either the Atlantic Ocean or the Gulf of Mexico. Most of the rivers that drain into the Gulf flow into the Mississippi River first.

THE HUDSON RIVER AND ERIE CANAL

The Hudson River starts high in the mountains of New York and flows south for 315 miles (507 kilometers) through New York City and into the Atlantic Ocean. The Hudson formed about 12,000 years ago when glaciers gouged out valleys. When the ice melted, the river began flowing.

In the early 1800s, most people lived along the East Coast. There was rich, fertile land farther west, but the Appalachian Mountains were a difficult barrier to cross. There was no easy way to transport goods across the mountains. People still needed cloth, tools, and other necessities from the East. Even today, it is much easier to transport goods by water than over land. Imagine how hard it was to move goods by land when there were no cars!

Finding a water route across the Appalachians would open up the West for settlement, but there weren't any water routes. Then some people had the idea of connecting the Hudson River to Lake Erie by building a water channel called a canal. No one had ever tried such a big construction project, and many people didn't like the idea. But others had vision and confidence, and on July 4, 1817, construction began.

In 1825, the Erie Canal opened, creating a river road that linked the Atlantic Ocean to the Great Lakes. The canal was 363 miles long (584 kilometers), anywhere from 28 to 40 feet wide (8½ to 12 meters), and 4 feet deep (1¼ meters). Because canal boats didn't have engines, horses and mules pulled them from tow paths along the sides of the canal. It took about 7 to 10 days to go from Erie, Pennsylvania, to Albany, New York. New Yorkers could now buy coal from western Pennsylvania and **crops** from Ohio and beyond. And Ohio farmers could buy manufactured goods. The Erie Canal is still used to ship goods, and it has been enlarged for larger boats.

Did You Know?

The Erie Canal took eight years to build. Men worked 14-hour days cutting down trees and digging by hand. The work was often dangerous, as they had to use gunpowder to blast open rock. Fevers often spread in the work camps.

NIAGARA FALLS

Niagara Falls are the most visited waterfalls in the world. What makes them so amazing? There is a huge volume of water that flows here from the Great Lakes, and the steep slope gives power to the raging water. There are many waterfalls in the world that are taller than Niagara or that carry more water, but Niagara Falls is among the top 10 in the world.

THE ERIE CANAL IN SONG

This classic folk song is about the Erie Canal. To save money, bridges across the canal were built just 4 feet above the water (1¼ meters), so when a boat got to a bridge, everyone called "Low Bridge! Everybody Down!"

I've got a mule, her name is Sal,
Fifteen miles on the Erie Canal.
She's a good ol' worker and a good ol' pal,
Fifteen miles on the Erie Canal.
We've hauled some barges in our day,
Filled with lumber, coal, and hay,
And we know every inch of the way,
From Albany to Buffalo.
Low bridge, everybody down!
Low bridge for we're comin' to a town!
And you'll always know your neighbor,
You'll always know your pal,
If you've ever navigated on the Erie Canal.

Niagara Falls are on the Niagara River in New York, which flows from Lake Erie to Lake Ontario. They are actually three sets of falls, two in New York called the American and Bridal Falls, and the Horseshoe Falls in Canada. The Horseshoe Falls drop 173 feet (53 meters) and the American Falls drop even farther at 183 feet (56 meters).

Did You Know?

No other very large waterfalls are as easily accessible as Niagara Falls. You can get right up close to Niagara Falls, see the falls from all angles, and even touch them!

The Horseshoe Falls, in a crescent shape, carry the most water and are the most spectacular.

Niagara Falls formed about 12,000 years ago. The entire region used to be covered by glaciers. As the glaciers moved, they dug out depressions in the land. Then, when temperatures rose and the ice melted, the depressions filled with water. These depressions became the Great Lakes and the Niagara River that joins Lake Erie and Lake Ontario.

The Niagara River flows over Niagara Falls. All rivers erode the rock they flow over. But some rocks under the Niagara River are harder than others, so they don't erode evenly.

The rocks at the top of Niagara Falls are harder than the softer rocks below. The softer rocks erode from underneath, which sometimes causes the harder rocks above to fall in large chunks. As a result, the waterfalls are slowly moving upstream as the rocks erode. But the waterfalls themselves don't disappear. They have moved about 7 miles (11 kilometers) upstream since they formed. There is now a **gorge** where Niagara Falls once was.

Did You Know?

It sounds crazy, but 21 people have attempted to go over Niagara Falls as a stunt. Sixteen of them have lived. People have gone over the Falls in a barrel, walked a tightrope across, or simply jumped.

RIVERS DRAINING INTO THE ATLANTIC OCEAN

There are several other important rivers that drain into the Atlantic Ocean.

• **The Connecticut River** is New England's largest river system, passing through Connecticut, Massachusetts, New Hampshire, and Vermont. It is 380 miles long (611 kilometers).

• **The Susquehanna** is the largest river completely in the United States that drains into the Atlantic. It is about 450 miles long and travels through Pennsylvania and Maryland (724 kilometers).

• **The Potomac River** flows through Virginia, West Virginia, Maryland, and Washington D.C. for 383 miles into Chesapeake Bay (616 kilometers). It winds past the Washington, Lincoln, and Jefferson Memorials in Washington D.C.

• **The James River** at 304 miles long (489 kilometers), was the first river given an English name. It was home to the first permanent English settlement, Jamestown. The James River is entirely in Virginia and is one of the longest rivers contained in one state.

THE LOWER MISSISSIPPI RIVER

The Mississippi River is one of the great rivers of the world. Including its tributaries, it's the largest river system in North America. It drains a huge area, including 31 states, from the Appalachian Mountains in the east, to the Rocky Mountains in the west, and north to Canada. The Lower Mississippi River is the part of the river starting from where the Ohio River joins it at Illinois, Kentucky, and Missouri, all the way to its **mouth** at the Gulf of Mexico.

WORDS TO KNOW

mouth: where a river empties into another body of water.

Rivers scour the land they flow over and pick up sediment that they carry downstream. The steeper and faster a river travels, the more sediment it can carry. But when that river reaches a body of water that is standing, such as the Gulf of Mexico, the water slows down and can't carry very much sediment. So the sediment drops and creates a new area of land called a river delta. Usually, a river delta is shaped like a fan.

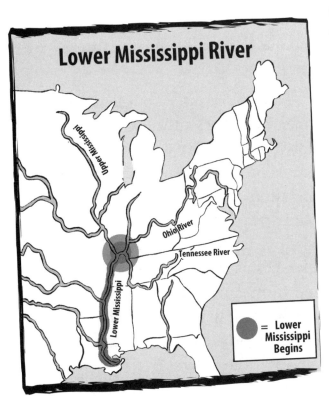

Did You Know?

The word "delta" describes the fan-shaped deposit of sediment at the mouth of a river. The name comes from the upper-case Greek letter Delta, which is shaped like a triangle.

83

As the Mississippi River nears the Gulf of Mexico, it drops much of the sediment that it's been carrying. That sediment has formed the land area called the Mississippi Delta, where the river breaks into smaller channels. The Mississippi carries about 145 million metric tons of **nutrient**-rich sediments from the interior of the country to the coastal region and the Gulf (2.4 billion kilograms).

Normally, a delta slowly increases in size as more sediments are deposited. But the Mississippi Delta is sinking below sea level because of dams and other man-made changes to the flow of the river. The Mississippi River used to carry more than twice the amount of sediments to the delta as it does today.

New Orleans, Louisiana, is a major **seaport** city about 100 miles upriver from the Gulf of Mexico (161 kilometers). The Army Corps of Engineers in New Orleans operates seven **dredges** that scour the bottom of the Mississippi to keep the channel at least 45 feet deep in this area (14 meters). This allows ocean-going ships to pass through New Orleans and upstream as far as Baton Rouge, Louisiana. New Orleans is the busiest seaport in the country. It also has the longest **wharf** in the world, which is 2 miles long and can fit 15 ships at one time (3½ kilometers).

WORDS TO KNOW

nutrients: substances that living things need to live and grow.

seaport: a place where ships can load and unload.

dredge: equipment that scoops up objects and mud from the bottom of a river or ocean.

wharf: a landing place where ships can tie up to load or unload.

Did You Know?

There are about 240 different kinds of fish in the Mississippi, along with about 50 different mammals. You can find egrets, muskrats, otters, and alligators in the mangrove swamps of the Lower Mississippi. The delta area is an important habitat for all kinds of fish and shellfish such as shrimp, oysters, and crab.

Did You Know?

Levees are man-made riverbanks built to prevent the river from overflowing its banks. They control the direction the river takes. There are more than 1,600 miles of levees along the Mississippi River, longer than the Great Wall of China! They protect the land from floods and keep the river in its main channel.

Up the river from New Orleans, the Army Corps of Engineers has constructed levees to keep most of the water in the main channel. Without the levees, the river would flow to the channel of the Atchafalaya River, which has steeper banks. If that happened, the amount of water combined would flood many areas where people live. The port of New Orleans would be left dry.

BARGES AND TOWS

All along the Mississippi, **barges** transport crops down the river to the port at New Orleans for transport all around the world. They also move coal, oil, and other goods up the river from the delta region and other parts of the world.

Barges are a better way to carry large loads than trucks or even trains. They use only one third as much fuel as a truck per ton of goods carried. Especially on the Lower Mississippi, many barges are pushed together by one towboat. About 30 barges are put together that carry up to about 45,000 tons of goods (40,800 metric tons). It would take 1,800 large trucks to carry all that. And some towboats can push as many as 70 barges together!

Levee

WORDS TO KNOW

barge: a flat-bottomed boat used to transport heavy loads on rivers or canals. A barge is pushed by a towboat.

OHIO RIVER

The Ohio River is the largest tributary of the mighty Mississippi River. In fact, where the Ohio joins the Mississippi, it's actually the larger of the two rivers. The Ohio starts in Pittsburgh, Pennsylvania, where the Allegheny and Monongahela Rivers join. It winds 981 miles (1,579 kilometers) until it reaches the Mississippi, twisting and turning along the way as it finds the lowest point.

Did You Know?

During the 1800s, a man from Massachusetts named John Chapman traveled up and down the Ohio River, planting apple seeds as he went. He planted so many apple trees that he was given the nickname, "Johnny Appleseed."

Native Americans, who built thousands of earth and stone mounds in the Ohio River valley, used the river as an important route for trading. Later, it served as a river road for Europeans transporting goods. The Ohio River still carries more goods by ship than any other river besides the Mississippi.

TENNESSEE RIVER

The Tennessee River is the largest tributary of the Ohio River,

about 652 miles long (1,049 kilometers). Like the Ohio, it's not that far from the Atlantic Ocean, but it drains west because the Appalachian Mountains block it from going east. It flows through Tennessee, Alabama, a bit of Mississippi, and Kentucky.

Do you live along the Tennessee River? Chances are that when you turn on the lights in your house, the energy is coming from power generated from the river.

How can water be turned into electricity? Actually, it isn't the water that is being turned into electricity. It's the energy from the strong flow of the water. A power plant that turns the energy from flowing water into electricity is called a hydroelectric plant because "hydro" means "water." The Tennessee River has many dams that are part of a system generating **hydroelectric energy**. Since water is a **renewable resource**, many people feel it is a better source of power than fossil fuels.

WORDS TO KNOW

hydroelectric energy: electricity generated from the energy of flowing water.

renewable resource: any natural resource that isn't used up, that can be replaced.

FLOOD!

A flood happens when water covers land that is usually dry. Heavy rain or snow can cause the water levels in a stream or river to rise high enough to flow over its banks. The Eastern Coast receives a lot of rain and snow, and floods can happen anywhere.

• The Johnstown Flood of 1889 flooded a small town on the floodplain of the Little Conemaugh and Stony Rivers in western Pennsylvania. There was a dam that created a lake on the Little Conemaugh. On May 31, 1889, the dam broke from heavy spring rains. Mud and water spewed out, destroying everything in its path and killing 2,209 people.

• The Mississippi River Flood of 1927 happened after heavy rains in 1926 left the Mississippi River water level high. When 15 inches of rain (31 centimeters) fell in 18 hours on April 15, 1927, the river overflowed its levees in 145 places. There were floods in 11 states, killing 246 people and causing $400 million in damages.

87

HOW HYDROELECTRIC ENERGY WORKS

For thousands of years, people have used water wheels to take the energy from flowing water and change it into mechanical energy to do work. Water wheels were often hooked up to huge grinding stones to grind wheat into flour. Hydroelectric power works in a similar way. But it transforms the energy into electricity instead of simply turning a grinding wheel.

Here's how it works:

1. A dam is built across the river to hold back all of the water. This creates a barrier across a river. The water backs up and forms a lake, called a reservoir.

2. The dam funnels the water into a large tunnel, called a penstock.

3. The penstock releases the water at a steady rate into huge turbines. A turbine is like a water wheel on its side, with large blades.

4. The flowing water turns the blades of the turbines. Then the water flows back into the river.

5. The turbine blades are connected to a large metal rod with giant, powerful magnets attached to it. The magnets spin very fast. They are surrounded by large coils of copper wire. When the magnets spin, they create electricity!

The amount of electricity that a hydroelectric plant can produce is determined by two things. One is the volume of water that flows through the turbines. The other is the height that the water falls from. The height from the reservoir to the turbines is called the head. When a lot of water falls from a great height, you can get a lot of electricity.

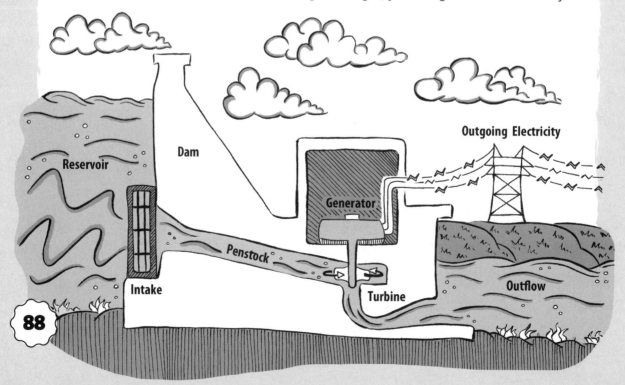

MAKE YOUR OWN
SWEET WATERFALL

1 Spray the whipped cream onto the plate in a square shape. Build up several layers until the whipped cream is about 1 inch high (2½ centimeters).

2 Break the chocolate bar into separate rectangles. Place the chocolate on top of the whipped cream in a single layer, with the rectangles touching each other.

3 Scoop out sections of whipped cream from underneath the chocolate. What happens to the chocolate? Of course, in the name of science, you'll have to eat the whipped cream and chocolate so you can continue to "erode" the whipped cream.

What's Happening?

The whipped cream is like soft rocks, capped by the harder chocolate rocks on top. As the water in a river erodes the soft rock, it undercuts the harder top layer, which falls down in chunks. This is what's happening when waterfalls, such as Niagara Falls, migrate upstream in a river.

MAKE YOUR OWN
RAFT

1 Place one piece of paper on a table. Place 10 popsicle sticks flat on the paper with their sides touching. This is your "raft."

2 Put dabs of glue onto both sides of another popsicle stick at one of its ends. Place this popsicle stick between the fifth and sixth popsicle sticks in your raft so it is standing upright. This is your "mast." Press the two sides of the raft together so they are snug against the mast and the glue.

3 Place beads of glue across the raft sticks in four lines. Two of the beads of glue should be close to the ends, and two beads of glue should be next to the mast.

4 Place the last four popsicle sticks on the beads of glue and press firmly. Let dry.

5 Cut a square from the second piece of paper about 4 inches square (10 centimeters). Glue it onto one of the flat sides of the mast at the top. You're ready to go rafting on the river!

SUPPLIES

- 2 sheets of paper
- 15 popsicle sticks
- glue
- scissors

Sail

X 4

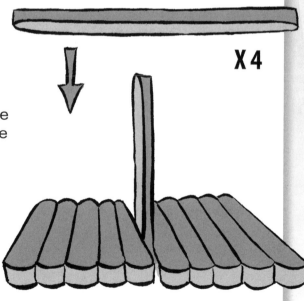

CHAPTER 7

ECOSYSTEMS

Water is the defining feature of the unique ecosystems in the Eastern Coast region. Freshwater forms lakes and ponds, and incredible, diverse wetlands throughout the region. These are low-lying areas of land such as a marshes or swamps, where the soil is soaked with water. Wetlands provide habitat for a wide variety of plants and animals. And salt water borders the entire East Coast, creating an environment that supports spectacular coral reefs and even more plants and animals.

THE EVERGLADES

The Everglades are one of the most important wetlands in the world. They stretch from Orlando, Florida, to the South Florida Bay. The Everglades are teeming with thousands of species of plants and animals, some of which aren't found anywhere else in the world.

You can find an amazing array of birds such as herons, ibis, and egrets. You can also find bears, foxes, panthers, alligators, manatees, and turtles.

Did You Know?

The Everglades is really a collection of several important ecosystems. The region has two seasons: the dry season from November to May, and the wet season from May to November. The ecosystems change considerably with the seasons. Many areas are marshy during the summer and much drier during the winter.

The best place to see the Everglades is in Everglades National Park. The park was created to preserve the incredible diversity of life in the Everglades. It is only a small part of the whole area occupied by the historic Everglades, but it is still a magnificent and diverse region. From a distance the park isn't very interesting, but up close, the park is fascinating.

SLOUGHS AND SAWGRASS MARSHES

At the heart of the Everglades is a river about 100 miles long (161 kilometers), 60 miles wide (97 kilometers), and about 6 inches deep in most places (15 centimeters). If that sounds like an unusually shallow and wide river, you're right. If you take a quick look, the water looks like a **stagnant** swamp. But the water is actually moving slowly, about 100 feet per day (30 meters).

The Everglades start at the huge Lake Okeechobee in central Florida, which is the largest freshwater lake in Florida, and the largest lake in the United States after the Great Lakes and the Great Salt Lake. The lake overflows its banks during the wet season, and flows south to Florida Bay.

WORDS TO KNOW

stagnant: not moving.
sawgrass: a tall grass in marshy areas, with leaves that have edges that look like the teeth of a saw.

There are free-flowing channels of water called sloughs (pronounced sloo). The two main sloughs are the Shark River Slough and the Taylor Slough. But most of the water in this huge river is filled with **sawgrass** that can grow up to 9 feet tall (3 meters). It grows right in the flow of water that goes through the Everglades, and gives the Everglades the nickname "River of Grass."

Scattered throughout the sloughs and sawgrass marshes are small islands of hardwood trees called hammocks. They are home to many species of small animals such as foxes, raccoons, and ducks.

CYPRESS SWAMPS

Cypress is a type of evergreen tree that can survive in a very wet environment. It doesn't need deep soil. Cypress swamps thrive throughout the Everglades, but are concentrated in the Big Cypress National Preserve on the north border of Everglades National Park. Some of the most fierce and ferocious animals in the country thrive here, like the American alligator and the Florida panther.

Did You Know?

Alligators and crocodiles only exist together in one place in the entire world—the Everglades! A group of alligators is called a congregation.

MANGROVE FORESTS

The Everglades has the most extensive system of mangrove forests in the world. Around the southern tip of Florida, the water runoff from Lake Okeechobee spreads out into smaller channels of **brackish** water. Lining these channels is a very peculiar type of tree—the mangrove. This tree lives directly in the water, but it has long, stilt-like roots that come out of the trunk a foot or two above the water (30 to 60 centimeters). These spidery roots absorb both salt and fresh water, and also help the tree "breathe" when its roots are covered by water. Mangrove forests provide a wall of protection against hurricanes and storm surges, since their unique roots make them extremely strong.

WORDS TO KNOW

brackish: slightly salty water that is a mix of seawater and river water.

The web of roots on mangroves also make an excellent place for fish and other marine life to make their nests. Mangrove forests are filled with a bounty of underwater life.

DON'T FORGET THE LITTLE GUYS!

The large animals that live in the Everglades, such as alligators, herons, and panthers, usually get the most attention. But they couldn't exist without the small animals they hunt, who couldn't exist without the many plants that grow in the Everglades. The most common plant is sawgrass, which carpets millions of acres. Geese and ducks feast on its seeds, and birds and **reptiles** nest in its thick hedges.

Many other water-dwelling plants live throughout the region, like bladderwort, white and yellow water lilies, and maidencane.

Though they have some strange names, you probably wouldn't notice anything special about any of these plants if you happened to see them in your backyard. If you hung around long enough though, you'd see the small, delicate, yellow bladderwort flower turn into a fierce hunter! When an insect hits a trigger on the bladderwort's petal, it is sucked into the flower. It all happens in about a hundredth of a second, making the bladderwort the fastest-known killer in the plant kingdom.

THE BIGGEST BEASTS IN THE EVERGLADES

Predators are an important part of any ecosystem. They hunt smaller animals, which helps to keep their populations balanced. Some of the most ferocious predators make their home in the Everglades.

WORDS TO KNOW

predator: an animal that hunts another animal for food.

extinction: the death of an entire species so that it no longer exists.

American Alligator: This is one impressive beast. On average, alligators measure from 10 to 15 feet from nose to tail (3 to 4½ meters), and can weigh up to 1,000 pounds (455 kilograms)! They are the largest reptile in North America. While alligators are clumsy on land, in the water they are lethal. Their webbed feet and powerful tails allow them to swim fast.

If you see a baby alligator or eggs, stay away. A mother alligator guards her eggs and her young ferociously! When the eggs hatch, the mother gently carries the hatchlings to the water in her mouth. Then she watches over her young for two years.

American alligators were hunted almost to **extinction**, and in 1967 the American alligator was named an endangered species. With protections in place, American alligators recovered fully, and today more than a million live across the southeastern United States. You might find them in rivers, marshes, or ponds—and of course they love the Everglades.

American Crocodile:
Sometimes the alligator is mistaken for its close relative, the American crocodile. This elusive animal only lives in one spot in the entire United States—the Everglades. There are a few differences between crocodiles and alligators.

- Crocodiles have a triangular head, while alligators have a broad, shorter snout.

- Crocodiles have lighter skin, while alligators have darker skin.

- The fourth tooth on the lower jaw of crocodiles is visible when their mouth is closed.

- Crocodiles are more rare, and live in salty or brackish water, while alligators live in fresh water.

Both animals are extremely powerful, and their bite is like being crushed by a small truck. And both are dangerous. Don't ever approach either an alligator or a crocodile, even if it looks asleep!

Florida Panther: If you're extremely lucky, you might see this rare and sneaky mammal on the prowl. The Florida Panther lives in southern Florida, with most of their population residing in Big Cypress National Preserve or Everglades National Park. Panthers can grow up to 7 feet long (2 meters), so they need a lot of space to roam and hunt. Each adult panther usually marks an area of about 200 square miles (322 square kilometers). Panthers are agile and fast, and can reach speeds of 35 miles per hour when hunting (56 kilometers per hour).

Florida Panthers were hunted almost to extinction. It's illegal to hunt them now, but a loss of habitat for the panthers makes it hard for them to thrive. In 1995 there were only about 20 to 30 Florida panthers left in existence. People have worked to help the panthers survive, and there are now about 100 panthers. That's a good start, but there's still a long way to go to ensure that the panther population is strong.

West Indian Manatee: The manatee is magnificent, and huge, but underneath it's a cuddly monster. This gentle giant munches on seagrass as it slowly paddles its way in shallow freshwater. Manatees can grow up to 10 feet long (3 meters) and weigh half a ton. They are often called "sea cows" because of the way they graze like cows. They are endangered, mainly because of a loss of habitat and accidental collisions with boats.

INVASIVE SPECIES

An **invasive species** is a plant or animal that is brought to a new ecosystem, either on purpose or by accident. It quickly multiplies to large numbers. Because the species isn't native to the area, there are no predators or diseases that naturally control its growth. So the species can spread quickly over a large area and overwhelm the **native species**. Several invasive species have made their home in the Everglades, disrupting the ecosystems. Some of the invasive plants are old-world climbing fern, melaleuca, seaside mahoe, and Brazilian pepper.

Invasive animals in the Everglades include the Burmese python and the green iguana.

The Burmese python is probably the most famous invasive species in the Everglades. In the 1980s, it became popular to keep these huge snakes as pets, but many pet owners later dumped them in the nearby Everglades. The large python has no predators in this ecosystem, so the population kept growing and growing. Unfortunately, the pythons eat 70 different rare and endangered species, bringing these species even closer to extinction. Hundreds of pythons are removed from the Everglades each year in an effort to control their numbers.

The green iguana is another reptile that has made a huge impact on the Everglades. This small, plant-eating reptile was also introduced to the ecosystem by careless pet owners. Some of the iguana's main food sources are two very rare plants that grow in the mangrove forests. If the iguana population continues to grow, these plant species may die out.

Before you get a pet—especially an unusual one—carefully consider whether you can take care of it. And if you already have a pet and find you can't care for it, don't just dump it into the wild! There are many places such as animal rescue organizations that can find a place for your pet.

Did You Know?

The Burmese python is one of the largest snake species on Earth, averaging 12 feet in length (3½ meters). Some grow as long as 19 feet (almost 6 meters). At times, they even eat alligators!

BAYOUS

A bayou is a body of slow-moving, sometimes stagnant water in a flat, low-lying area. Bayous are found mainly on the Gulf Coast in the states of Texas, Alabama, Louisiana, Mississippi, Arkansas, and southern Florida. The Gulf Coast region of the East Coast is perfect for bayous because of the many rivers, streams, and other bodies of water that branch off of larger rivers like the Mississippi. Many different species make their home in the bayou, like catfish, frogs, alligators, crawfish, and shrimp. The East Coast has some well-known bayous.

Did You Know?

The Great Dismal Swamp is a marshy area in southern Virginia and northern North Carolina. It's one of the largest wild areas left in the East Coast region. Lake Drummond lies in its center, and the entire area is home to an incredible variety of wildlife, including birds, bears, weasels, bobcats, and otters. During early American history, escaped slaves formed a settlement in the Great Dismal Swamp.

WORDS TO KNOW

reef: an area of rocks, coral, or sand that is close to the surface of the water.

Bayou Teche used to be the main course of the Mississippi River until about 2,800 years ago, when the river switched its course.

Bayou Bartholomew is the longest bayou in the world, measuring 364 miles long (586 kilometers), and stretching between Louisiana and Arkansas. It has at least 117 species of fish and 31 species of mussels, which makes it the most diverse stream in North America for aquatic animals.

CORAL REEFS

Coral **reefs** are the most diverse ecosystems in all the oceans, and are built by animals smaller than your fingernail. They form where the water is warm and clear. The tiny coral animals just need a solid structure to attach to. Florida is the only state in the continental United States that has extensive coral reefs. These reefs provide food, shelter, and breeding places for a huge variety of plants and animals. You might find lobsters, snapper, crabs, shrimp, and sharks swimming around the coral reefs off of the southern tip of Florida, taking advantage of the wide array of life that flourishes there. Florida has many different reef-building corals.

Brain Coral is a massive, round coral that has curved grooves on its surface that look like the folds of a human brain. Brain coral grows slowly, but is very sturdy.

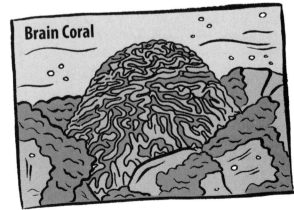
Brain Coral

Star Coral is the most common coral in deeper water. It has a star pattern on its surface.

Elkhorn Coral has large, flattened branches that look remarkably like the horns of an elk or moose. It grows fairly quickly—several inches in a year (more than 10 centimeters).

Staghorn Coral's cylindrical branches can grow to anywhere from a few inches to over 6 feet long (10 centimeters to 2 meters).

Dry Tortugas National Park is a cluster of seven islands about 70 miles west of Key West, Florida (113 kilometers). The islands are made of coral reefs and sand. Tropical storms often shift and reform the sand. Dry Tortugas has incredible birds and marine plants and animals, as well as about 30 species of coral.

Dry Tortugas National Park is part of the Great Florida Reef. This huge barrier reef is 170 miles long and 4 miles wide (274 kilometers long and 6½ kilometers wide). A barrier reef is a long reef that creates a barrier between a coastline and the ocean. The Great Florida Reef is the third-largest barrier reef in the world, and is about 6,000 years old. Like other coral reefs, the Great Florida Reef has suffered damage in recent decades from diseases and changes in water temperature. Many organizations work to protect the reef, to keep the ecosystem healthy enough to support the millions of animals that live there.

MAKE YOUR OWN
NAKED EGGS

1 Place your eggs in the bowl. Try to keep the eggs from touching each other. Fill the bowl with enough vinegar to cover the eggs. Set the bowl where you can see it but where it will be undisturbed. Cover it if the vinegar smell bothers you.

SUPPLIES

- a few whole eggs, still in their shells
- bowl
- vinegar

2 After at least a day, carefully take out the eggs. They should be soft and you may be able to see through them a bit. If the eggs aren't soft, pour out the old vinegar, put the eggs back in the bowl, and cover with new vinegar for another day or so. You may also see a chalky white layer on the outside. If the egg is soft, you can gently rub this off under running water. This is what's left of the shell.

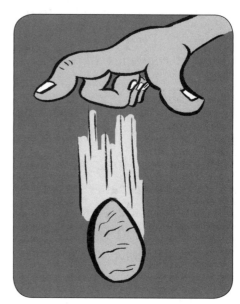

3 Hold one of the naked eggs a few inches above the kitchen sink and drop it (about 10 centimeters). From how high can you drop an egg before it breaks?

What's Happening?

Eggshells are made mostly of calcium carbonate, a naturally occurring substance produced by coral to form coral reefs. Seashells, pearls, limestone, and eggshells are made of calcium carbonate. The egg actually grows the mineral shell. Vinegar is an acid, and calcium carbonate is a **base**. When the vinegar and eggshell come into contact, they react and the vinegar dissolves the shell.

Corals use calcium and other particles called carbonate ions in seawater to make the calcium carbonate skeletons they live in. When coral dies, its skeleton remains and new coral builds on the old skeleton. This is how a coral reef grows.

In some parts of the world today, coral reefs are threatened. Ocean water is basic. But there are some places where seawater is becoming slightly less basic and coral reefs are suffering. If water is less basic, it means there are fewer carbonate ions for corals to use to make their skeletons. Increased carbon dioxide in the atmosphere from human activity may be causing this change.

The ocean will never be as acidic as the vinegar in your experiment, but it may not always be basic enough. Scientists are researching how the atmosphere, oceans, and coral reefs work together, so we can make sure coral has what it needs to live and grow.

CHAPTER 8

THE COAST

The Eastern Coast region has more coastline than any other region in America. From Maine to Florida, wrapping around the Gulf Coast to Louisiana, 17 different states border the ocean. The coast might seem like a simple border between the land and water, but it's a complex place for people, plants, and animals.

The Atlantic Ocean isn't the same everywhere. There are big differences from place to place, such as temperature and the types of plants and animals living there. Some of these differences have to do with the currents, and the major inlets of Chesapeake Bay in Maryland and the Gulf of Mexico.

THE GULF STREAM

All oceans have currents, which are big movements of water over hundreds and thousands of miles. They're a bit like an underwater river. The major currents in the Northern Hemisphere move in a clockwise direction. This is the reason for one of the world's major ocean currents: the Gulf Stream.

The Gulf Stream is a current that starts in the Gulf of Mexico and travels north up the east coast to Cape Hatteras, North Carolina. Then the current moves away from North America as it heads into the Atlantic Ocean and toward Europe. The Gulf Stream carries more water than all of the world's rivers combined!

Because the Gulf Stream starts in the warm, tropical waters of the Gulf of Mexico, it makes the places it travels to warmer than they would be otherwise. For example, London, England, is farther north than cities in the state of Maine. But average winter temperatures in Maine are several degrees colder because the Gulf Stream doesn't go there.

Gulf Stream

The Gulf Stream also makes the southeast coast of the United States, including Florida, Georgia, South Carolina, and North Carolina, warmer than you might expect.

The Gulf Stream is one of the fastest ocean currents. It travels at an average speed of 4 miles per hour (6½ kilometers per hour), but can go as fast as 5½ miles per hour at the surface (9 kilometers per hour). That's faster than people walk, and is many times faster than the speed of the Amazon River!

GULF OF MEXICO

The Gulf of Mexico is a major body of water that is connected to the Atlantic Ocean. It is enclosed by the states of Florida, Alabama, Mississippi, Louisiana, Texas, and the countries of Mexico and Cuba. About half of the Gulf is relatively shallow because the continental shelf reaches out along much of its coast. The continental shelf is an extension of the continent that is covered by water. Water in the continental shelf might be only tens of feet or meters deep, compared to the deep ocean, which is thousands of feet or meters deep.

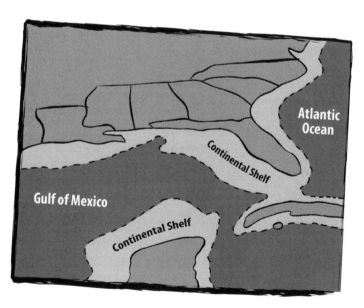

Because so much of the Gulf of Mexico is fairly shallow, it has a lot of plants and animals living on its ocean floor.

There is always more life in shallower water than in deeper oceans where it is dark and the water pressure is very strong. The Gulf is full of fish of all kinds: snapper, swordfish, grouper, shrimp, crabs, and oysters. More fish and shellfish are harvested from the Gulf each year than from the mid-Atlantic Ocean and Chesapeake Bay combined.

OLD SOW

Old Sow is an enormous **whirlpool** that sometimes forms off the coast between Maine and Canada. Old Sow forms because of the unusual shape of the underwater seafloor. Many ships have been lost in its depths, especially before boats had motors. The whirlpool can be as large as 250 feet across (75 meters)!

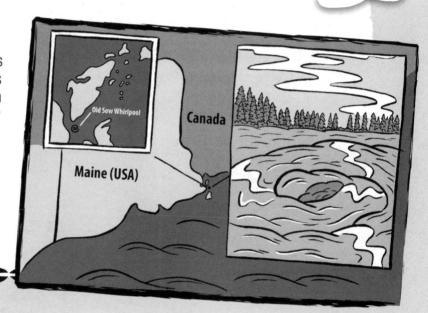

Old Sow Whirlpool

Canada

Maine (USA)

CHESAPEAKE BAY

Chesapeake Bay is a large **estuary**, where salt water from the ocean mixes with freshwater from rivers. Its watershed covers Maryland, Virginia, West Virginia, Delaware, Pennsylvania, and New York. Chesapeake Bay formed about 12,000 years ago when glaciers melted, causing the sea level to rise. The rising seawater flooded the area.

WORDS TO KNOW

whirlpool: a current of water spinning in a circle.

estuary: a partly enclosed coastal body of water, which has rivers and streams flowing into it and is connected to the ocean.

Because of the mixing of fresh and salt water, and because it's protected from large ocean storms, Chesapeake Bay is the perfect place for huge numbers of plants and animals to live.

107

There are over 2,700 different kinds of plants and animals living in the bay. If you want to try crabbing, Chesapeake Bay is the place to go! Some of the animals you might find there include:

- Chesapeake Bay blue crabs
- Atlantic bottlenose dolphins
- muskrats
- bobcats
- red foxes
- bald eagles
- ospreys
- great blue herons
- oysters
- hermit crabs
- horseshoe crabs

One of the most important elements of Chesapeake Bay is its submerged aquatic vegetation. These underwater grasses provide food and shelter for many organisms in the bay. The more than 16 species of underwater grasses include wild celery, sago pondweed, redhead grass, and water stargrass.

Did You Know?

Chesapeake Bay is the largest estuary in the United States. The Susquehanna River provides half of the freshwater coming into the bay.

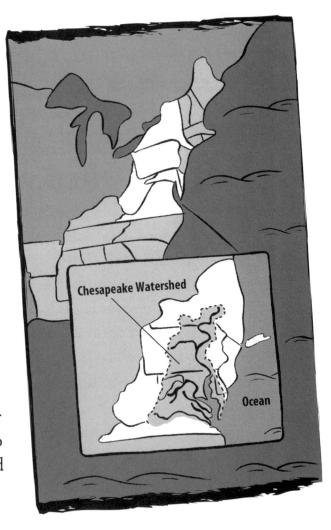

Chesapeake Watershed

Ocean

These grasses provide important places for young crabs and fish to hide from predators. Many birds eat the bay grasses, and the grasses also help prevent erosion.

Chesapeake Bay has suffered from pollution and overfishing in the past, but it has been improving in recent years.

Human activity causes sediments and nutrients to flow into the bay. Most of these nutrients come from fertilizers used by farmland and from towns and cities. You might think that nutrients would be good for the bay, but too many nutrients are a problem. Algae grows when there are too many nutrients, and excessive algae use up the oxygen in the water. This makes it difficult for other living things to survive.

Did You Know?

Chesapeake Bay in Maryland holds more than 18 trillion gallons of water. Most of the bay is less than 6 feet deep (1.8 meters). There's about 11,600 miles of shoreline, which is more than the entire West Coast (more than 18,600 kilometers)!

Overfishing has also reduced the number of fish, crabs, and other shellfish that live in the bay. People have been working to reduce pollution and to limit the harvesting of fish and shellfish. This will help the bay to recover its populations of plants and animals.

BEACHES AND ROCKY COASTS

When most people think of the coast, they think of miles of sandy beaches. The Eastern Coast certainly has beaches, but it also has rocky coasts, wetlands, and coral reefs. The wetlands mix with the beaches

all along the coast, as well as in bays such as Chesapeake Bay. Scuba diving is a fun activity among the coral reefs that can be found on the Florida coast.

Beaches extend from Massachusetts to Louisiana. There are long stretches of sugary sand, and short sandy stretches mixed in with other areas. Beaches usually form where there is a wide continental shelf and little tectonic activity, which is true on the Atlantic and Gulf Coasts.

Beaches are made of sand that is constantly in motion.

Waves, tides, and currents move the sand, and the beaches can change from day to day. They form from sediments that are carried from inland areas by rivers and wind, as well as from the ocean bottom. Beaches along the Eastern Coast usually have dunes on the inland side. Strong dune grasses anchor the sand in place. The dunes are an important environment for wildlife and other plants.

Along the Atlantic and Gulf Coasts, narrow barrier islands have formed parallel to the coast in many places. They protect the coast from storms and powerful waves, and form complex systems with marshes, dunes, and inlets.

BALD HEAD ISLAND

Bald Head Island is a barrier island off the coast of North Carolina. You can reach Bald Head Island only by ferry. Once on the island, you can only get around by foot, bicycle, or golf carts. Bald Head is a mix of beaches, with a marsh and a forest that run through the island. Some of the wildlife on the island include red and gray foxes, coyotes, and otters. Along the marshes, look for loons, peregrine falcons, egrets, and great blue herons. In the many freshwater lagoons, you might even see an American alligator!

From May through October, loggerhead sea turtles nest all along the coast from North Carolina to Florida, including at Bald Head Island. Loggerheads are about 3 feet long (about 1 meter) and have an extra big head. They eat crabs and other animals with hard shells, as well as fish and seaweed. Loggerheads are an endangered species because many of them are caught in fishing nets, and development in their nesting areas has reduced the numbers of turtles that hatch. People are trying to protect loggerheads by using fishing gear that doesn't catch turtles, and by protecting nesting areas.

A female returns to nest at the same place that she herself hatched. She may travel thousands of miles to reach that special place. She climbs up onto the beach and digs a deep hole for the eggs with her flippers. After the eggs hatch, the baby turtles dig their way up through the sand. The hatchlings are only about 2 inches long (5 centimeters). They head for the ocean quickly to escape from predators like crabs and birds. At night they scurry toward the brightest light, which is usually the moonlight shining on the ocean. Artificial lights can confuse the hatchlings about which way to go, so people who live along beaches are trying to reduce their use of lights at night.

Did You Know?

Cape Fear is a narrow piece of land that sticks out into the ocean from Bald Head Island in North Carolina. It gets its name for a reason. The Cape Fear River and the Gulf Stream come together here, and the mixing currents create dangerous waters. Off the coast of the island are 30 miles of dangerous waters and sand bars (48 kilometers), called the Frying Pan Shoals.

LIGHTHOUSES

Rocky shores on the Eastern Coast have formed where glaciers and strong waves have removed the fine-grained sediment from a coast. In Maine and other parts of New England, the glaciers retreated quickly and didn't leave much sediment behind.

WORDS TO KNOW

harbor: a protected indent in a coastline where ships can anchor and unload.

Lighthouses warn ships of dangerous coastlines and help guide them along the coast and into safe **harbors**. This tall tower with a light must be high enough to be seen from far away. Each lighthouse has its own pattern of flashing on and off, and sometimes even a colored light. At night, a ship captain knows where he is by the pattern of the lights. The shape of the lighthouse and its colors and patterns of paint is called its day mark.

Lighthouses were used as far back as ancient Egypt and China. In the year 283, the Egyptians built the tallest lighthouse in history. It stood 900 feet tall (274 meters) and worked for 1,500 years. The first lighthouse in North America was built in St. Augustine, Florida, in 1586. The oldest lighthouse in the United States that still exists is the Sandy Hook Lighthouse in New Jersey. It was built in 1764, and it's still in operation! The United States has a long coastline, with more lighthouses than any other nation.

ACADIA

Acadia National Park is a cluster of islands on the Maine coast. Like much of the northern Atlantic coast in Maine and Canada, the park has a rocky shoreline. The tides bring in water twice a day. When the tides go out, some of the water stays behind in tide pools, which are bustling with plants and animals. This area is called the intertidal zone because it is exposed between the tides. Creatures have to be very resourceful to live in this area because sometimes they are covered in seawater, and other times exposed to air. Some of the creatures that live in tide pools are barnacles, sea stars, mussels, crabs, and sea cucumbers.

Before electricity, lighthouses were lit using fires. Later the lamps were fueled by oil. A lighthouse keeper was responsible for tending the lighthouse, which included adding the fuel, winding clocks, maintaining the lighthouses, and weathering storms. They usually lived in a small house attached to the lighthouse, often in remote and lonely locations. Lighthouse keepers sometimes risked their lives to rescue people from ships that sank during storms.

In 1907, the Swedish inventor Nils Dalén developed a "solar valve" that shut off the light at sunrise. The valve relit the light if it was cloudy or foggy, and at night. With this invention, lighthouses could work more efficiently. Dalén received the Nobel Prize in physics for this work in 1912.

Of course, everything is automated now and lighthouse keepers aren't needed anymore. Many lighthouses aren't even needed anymore because ship captains have GPS and other ways of knowing where they are.

MAKE YOUR OWN
LIGHTHOUSE

1 Using the pencil, draw the outline shown here on the paper. Make the shape as big as you can. Outline the stripes, but don't color them in yet.

2 Cut out the shape. Roll the paper into a cone-shape tower that is narrower at the top but with an opening wide enough for the bottom of the plastic cup to fit inside. Slide one edge underneath the opposite edge. Make sure the lines for the stripes meet. If they don't, slightly redraw the lines so they do.

Color Black

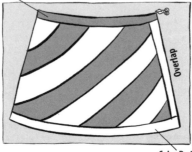

Overlap

Color Red

3 Unroll the paper and lay it flat. Color the bottom edge red and the top edge black. Then color in the diagonal stripes black.

4 Roll the paper back up and tape it closed, making sure the stripes meet and one edge is underneath the other. You can color a bit more with black marker to help the stripes meet.

5 Insert the bottom of the plastic cup into the top of the tower. The top of the cup should stick out. Tape the cup to the paper tower.

6 On the black paper, trace around the large glass to make a circle. Cut out the circle, then cut a straight line from the outside of the circle to the center. Overlap the two cut edges slightly to form a cone shape. Tape the edges. Tape the cone on top of the clear plastic cup so that it looks like a hat.

7 Roll a ball of clay and flatten it slightly. Press the bottom of the flashlight into the clay so that the flashlight can stand upright. Turn it on and place the paper tower over the flashlight.

Plastic Cup

What's Happening?

The Cape Hatteras Lighthouse is the tallest and one of the best-known lighthouses in America. It is located on Hatteras Island in the Outer Banks of North Carolina. It is 208 feet tall (63 meters), and was constructed from about 1,250,000 bricks. This region was known as the "Graveyard of the Atlantic" because so many ships sank in the ocean storms in the area. The Gulf Stream collides with colder water from the north here, which makes for treacherous waters. The Cape Hatteras light is visible every 7.5 seconds and can be seen for up to 24 miles under clear conditions (39 kilometers). Its day mark is a diagonal black and white stripe, similar to a barbershop pole—just like the one you made.

MAKE YOUR OWN
CORIOLIS EFFECT

SUPPLIES

- white posterboard or large sheet of paper
- scissors
- friend
- marker

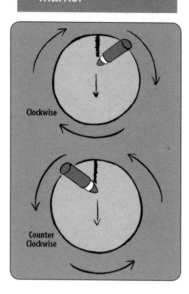

Clockwise

Counter Clockwise

1 Cut the posterboard into a circle. Hold it against the wall by pressing your finger in the center of the circle. Press hard enough to hold the paper against the wall but so that the paper can turn freely. Have your friend practice spinning the paper clockwise. The paper should turn at a steady rate.

2 While your friend is turning the paper, take the marker in your other hand. Draw from top to bottom on the paper in a straight line through the center.

3 Take down the paper and turn it over. Switch places and do the same thing, but this time turn the paper counterclockwise. Take down your paper and look at both sides. Are the lines straight?

What's Happening?

Winds and currents of water are affected by the Coriolis effect. When you turned the paper clockwise, the movement of the line curved to the left. This is how motion occurs in the Southern Hemisphere as the globe rotates from west to east. When you turned the paper counterclockwise, it was like the motion in the Northern Hemisphere, and the line curved to the right. Hurricanes in the Northern Hemisphere move west and up the Eastern Coast due to the Coriolis effect. It's also why the Gulf Stream travels north along the Eastern Coast, then out into the Atlantic.

acidic: from acids, which are chemical compounds that taste sour. Examples are vinegar and lemon juice. Water also contains some acid.

adapt: changes a plant or animal makes to survive.

albino: a human, animal, or plant that is very pale and does not have the usual amount of skin, eye, and hair color.

altitude: the elevation, or height above sea level.

asthenosphere: the semi-molten middle layer of the earth that includes the lower mantle. Much of the asthenosphere flows slowly, like Silly Putty.

atmosphere: the air surrounding the earth.

barge: a flat-bottomed boat used to transport heavy loads on rivers or canals. A barge is pushed by a towboat.

base: a substance with a bitter taste. Soap is usually a base. So is baking soda and ammonia.

bayou: a term used mainly in Mississippi and Louisiana for the swampy arm or slow-moving outlet of a lake.

bedrock: solid rock under loose material such as soil, sand, clay, or gravel.

biodiversity: the range of living things in an area.

blizzard: a severe snow storm with high winds, low temperatures, and heavy snow.

brackish: slightly salty water that is a mix of seawater and river water.

brittle: describes a solid that breaks when put under pressure. A blade of grass will bend, but a dry twig is brittle and will break.

carbon: an element found in all living things.

carbon dioxide: a gas formed by the rotting of plants and animals, and when animals breathe out.

cave: a natural underground opening connected to the surface, large enough for a person to enter.

cavern: a very large cave or system of interconnected caves.

chasm: a deep crack or hole.

climate: the average weather of an area over a long period of time.

coal: a dark brown or black rock formed from decayed plants. Coal is used as a fuel.

coastal plain: a flat area that is bound by the sea on one side and an area of higher elevation on the other side.

continental: relating to the earth's large land masses.

continental shelf: the border of a continent that slopes gradually under water.

convergent boundary: where two plates come together.

core: the center of the earth, composed of the metals iron and nickel. The core has a solid inner core and a liquid outer core.

crop: a plant grown for food and other uses.

crust: the thick, outer layer of the earth.

current: a constantly moving mass of liquid.

dense: tightly packed.

divergent boundary: where two plates are moving in opposite directions, sometimes called a rift zone. New crust forms at rift zones from the magma pushing through the crust.

dredge: equipment that scoops up objects and mud from the bottom of a river or ocean.

earthquake: a sudden movement in the outer layer of the earth. It releases stress built up from the motion of the earth's plates.

ecosystem: a community of plants and animals living in the same area and relying on each other to survive.

elevation: height above sea level.

endangered: a kind of plant or animal that is at risk of disappearing entirely.

equator: an imaginary line around the earth, halfway between the North and South Poles.

erosion: the wearing away and carrying off of materials on the earth's surface.

eruption: a violent explosion of gas, steam, or ash.

estuary: a partly enclosed coastal body of water, which has rivers and streams flowing into it and is connected to the ocean.

evaporate: when a liquid heats up and changes into a gas.

extinction: the death of an entire species so that it no longer exists.

fault: a crack in the outer layer of the earth.

fertile: land that is good for growing plants.

floodplain: an area around a shallow winding river where the land is lower than other areas.

fossil fuels: oil, natural gas, and coal, which are natural fuels that formed long ago from the remains of living organisms.

fossil: the remains or traces of ancient plants or animals.

geography: the study of the earth and its features, especially the shape of the land, and the effect of human activity on the earth.

geologist: a scientist who studies the earth and its movements.

geology: the scientific study of the history and physical nature of the earth.

geyser: a liquid shooting high into the air.

glacial period: a period of time within an ice age when a large part of the earth's surface is covered with ice.

glaciation: when a large part of the earth is covered in ice.

glacier: a huge mass of ice and snow.

gorge: a narrow valley between hills or mountains, usually with steep rocky walls and a stream running through it.

habitat: the natural area where a plant or animal lives.

harbor: a protected indent in a coastline where ships can anchor and unload.

horizontal drilling: drilling for oil or gas where the well is horizontal or close to horizontal.

hotspot: an area in the middle of a plate, where hot magma rises to the surface.

hurricane: a severe tropical storm with winds greater than 74 miles per hour.

hydraulic fracturing: a process where liquids are pumped down a well at high pressure to force the surrounding rock to fracture, or crack.

hydroelectric energy: electricity generated from the energy of flowing water.

hydrosphere: the earth's water, including oceans, rivers, lakes, glaciers, and water vapor in the air.

Ice Age: a period of time when large ice sheets cover large areas of land. It particularly refers to the most recent series of glaciations during the Pleistocene. An ice age can include shorter periods when glaciers retreat, as well as periods when the glaciers grow.

igneous rock: rock that forms from cooling magma.

interglacial period: a period within an ice age that is somewhat warmer and glaciers retreat.

invasive species: a species that is not native to an ecosystem and rapidly expands to crowd out other species.

larvae: the wormlike stage of an insect's life.

latitude: the lines that run west and east on the globe parallel to the equator. Latitudes vary from zero degrees at the equator to 90 degrees at the North and South Poles.

limestone: a type of rock that often forms from the shells of sea animals.

lithosphere: the rigid outer layer of the earth that includes the crust and the upper mantle.

low pressure: a pocket of air in the atmosphere that is not pushing down strongly toward Earth.

magma: partially melted rock below the surface of the earth.

mantle: the middle layer of the earth. The upper mantle, together with the crust, forms the lithosphere.

metamorphic rock: rock that has been transformed by heat or pressure or both into new rock, while staying solid.

microbes: a huge variety of living creatures that are so small they can only be seen with a microscope.

mine: to dig something out of the ground.

molten: melted by heat to form a liquid.

mouth: where a river empties into another body of water.

native species: a species that belongs in an ecosystem.

natural gas: a colorless, odorless gas used as a fuel.

Nor'easter: a storm blowing from the northeast, usually along the northeastern coast of the United States. It often brings high winds and cold temperatures.

Northern Hemisphere: the half of the earth north of the equator. The southern half is called the Southern Hemisphere.

nutrients: substances that living things need to live and grow.

oceanic: in or from the ocean.

oil: a thick dark liquid that occurs naturally beneath the earth. Oil can be separated into many products, including gasoline and other fuels.

old-growth forest: a forest that is very old.

organic material: matter that has come from organisms.

organism: any living thing.

plain: a large area of flat land.

plateau: a large, raised area that is fairly flat.

plate tectonics: the theory that describes how plates move across the earth and interact with each other to produce earthquakes, volcanoes, and mountains.

precipitation: rain, snow, or any form of water falling to Earth.

predator: an animal that hunts another animal for food.

raw material: a material that can be used to make a new or useful product.

reef: an area of rocks, coral, or sand that is close to the surface of the water.

renewable resource: any natural resource that isn't used up, that can be replaced.

reptile: a cold-blooded animal such as a snake, lizard, alligator, or turtle, that has a spine, lays eggs, has scales or horny places, and breathes air.

Richter scale: a scale used to measure the strength of an earthquake.

rifting: when the lithosphere splits apart.

sawgrass: a tall grass in marshy areas, with leaves that have edges that look like the teeth of a saw.

seaport: a place where ships can load and unload.

sedimentary rock: rock formed from the compression of sediments, the remains of plants and animals, or from the evaporation of seawater.

sediment: loose rock particles such as sand and clay.

seismic wave: a wave of energy generated from an earthquake. The wave travels through the earth.

seismograph: an instrument that measures the intensity of a seismic wave.

sinkhole: a hole or depression in the land, normally caused by erosion in the underlying rock. Sinkholes can swallow cars or even homes.

slave: a person owned by another person and forced to work without pay, against their will.

species: a group of plants or animals that are related and look like each other.

speleothem: a distinctive cave formation, such as a stalactite or stalagmite.

stagnant: not moving.

subduction: when one tectonic plate slides underneath another tectonic plate.

subtropical: an area close to the tropics where the weather is warm.

technology: tools, methods, and systems used to solve a problem or do work.

tectonic: relating to the forces that produce movement and changes in the earth's crust.

trade winds: steady winds that blow from east to west in a belt between 30 degrees latitude above the equator to 30 degrees latitude below the equator.

transform boundary: where two plates slide against each other.

tropical: a hot climate, usually near the equator.

tropical storm: a revolving storm that forms in the tropics.

volcano: a vent in the earth's surface through which magma, ash, and gases erupt.

watershed: the land area that drains into a river or stream.

water vapor: water as a gas, like steam or mist.

wharf: a landing place where ships can tie up to load or unload.

whirlpool: a current of water spinning in a circle.

BOOKS

Anderson, Alan, Gwen Diehn, and Terry Krautwurst. *Geology Crafts for Kids: 50 Nifty Projects to Explore the Marvels of Planet Earth.* New York: Sterling, 1998.

Blobaum, Cindy and Michael Kline. *Geology Rocks! 50 Hands-On Activities to Explore the Earth.* Vermont: Williamson Publishing Company, 1999.

Carson, Mary Kay. I*nside Hurricanes (Inside Series).* New York: Sterling, 2010.

Challoner, Jack. *Hurricane & Tornado* (DK Eyewitness Books). New York: DK Children, 2004.

Farndon, John. *How the Earth Works.* New York: Dorling Kindersley Publishers Ltd, 1999.

Geore, Michael. *Glaciers.* Mankato, Minnesota: Creative Education, Inc., 1991.

Nadeau, Isaac. *Glaciers.* New York: Powerkids Press, 2006.

WEB SITES

- **www.maps.google.com** Satellite view of the Eastern Coast Region. Click on the Satellite tab and scroll to wherever you want to look. You can zoom in or out.

- **www.nps.gov** National Park Service main web site. Click on links to find specific national parks and monuments such as Everglades National Park.

- **www.42explore.com/mining.htm** Cool information about mining, caves, hurricanes, Mississippi River.

- **pubs.usgs.gov/sim/2830/** Beautiful, detailed maps by the U.S. Geologic Society of the Appalachian Mountains and tectonic events.

- **mineralsciences.si.edu/tdpmap/** World Interactive Map of Volcanoes, Earthquakes, Impact Craters, and Plate Tectonics, by Smithsonian, USGS, and US Naval Research Laboratory.

- **earthquake.usgs.gov/earthquakes/** Earthquakes in all states.

- **earthquake.usgs.gov/learn/kids/** U.S. Geological Survey (U.S.G.S.) Earthquakes for Kids site.

- **www.energyquest.ca.gov/story/chapter08.html** Information about coal, oil, and natural gas.

- **www.eia.gov/kids/index.cfm** Kids website about renewable and nonrenewable energy sources.

- **www.nature.nps.gov/geology/caves/index.htm** Information on caves and karst topography, especially in the National Parks.

- **www.usatoday.com/weather/resources/askjack/archives-weather-extremes.htm** Questions and Answers about Weather facts.

- **earthobservatory.nasa.gov/NaturalHazards/view.php?id=15399** A 3-D cut-away model of Hurricane Katrina. Click on the link for an animation.

- **www.americanrivers.org/about-rivers/** Facts about rivers, dams, river songs, and more.

- **water.usgs.gov/** Water resources in the U.S.

- **kids.nationalgeographic.com/kids/animals/creaturefeature/american-alligator/** Information and images on American alligators.

- **www.dep.state.fl.us/coastal/habitats/coral/** Information on Florida's coral reefs.

INDEX

121